Overcoming Com

Overcoming Common Problems Series

Overcoming Common Problems

Coping with Teenagers

Sarah Lawson

First published in Great Britain in 2003 by
Sheldon Press
1 Marylebone Road
London NW1 4DU

British Library Cataloguing-in-Publication Data

A catalogue record for this book is available from the British Library

ISBN 0–85969–902–1

1 3 5 7 9 10 8 6 4 2

Typeset by Deltatype Limited, Birkenhead, Merseyside
Printed in Great Britain by Biddles Ltd
www.biddles.co.uk

For Bob

Contents

Acknowledgements

When they heard that I was writing about teenagers, almost everyone I met had a story to tell me. Some of them appear in this book; many didn't make it into print, but made me think or laugh. Thank you to all of you.

Thanks, also, to my tireless proof-reader, Bob Stephenson, my ICT adviser, David Harris, and my own four children – Jo, Chris, Izzy and Callum. They are living proof that teenagers can be responsible, kind, loving friends, and I know very well how lucky I am to be their mum.

Introduction

At some point in our history, the significance and promise of becoming an adolescent was lost, to be replaced, in the early 1950s, by the dubious concept of the 'teenager' – an awkward, truculent individual with a propensity for getting into trouble and causing his parents heartache.

It wasn't always like this. Many centuries ago, when we were still a tribal people (and to this day in many tribal societies), the transition from childhood to adolescence was an occasion for ritual and celebration. The young boy's first hunt or battle, and the girl's first period, marked their initiation into the adult world. More was expected of them, but their new status was honoured by the tribe and they were expected to fulfil their duties as adults: to exercise their new rights and privileges responsibly, alongside – and with the support of – their elders.

Things changed with the start of the Industrial Revolution. Before this, in what was a largely agricultural economy, children worked alongside their parents on the family farm or smallholding, contributing materially to the welfare of all; we still have a long school holiday in summer because country children simply didn't go to school during the busiest time of year on the farm – the period of haymaking and harvest. The shift of employment from the home or local community into factories and offices and the introduction of compulsory education up to 14, and then 16, years of age, however, ended all this. Most adolescents now spend little time in the company of their parents or other adults, and few have the opportunity to contribute to their family's income or welfare.

There have been advantages to children from their exclusion from the workplace, of course – they no longer work long hours in factories, or die up chimneys, or down mines; every child has access to a basic education and the opportunity to progress to higher education if he wishes to – and if his parents can afford to support him through his studies. Nevertheless, there have been losses, too, particularly where the young person approaching sexual maturity is concerned.

INTRODUCTION

The adolescent is no longer a child. It is his nature to seek
out new experiences; to find independence from his parents and
break new ground; to find a personality and a direction for
himself, make his mark on the world, and establish himself as
an adult. He is reactive and enthusiastic, passionate and eager to
learn, full of curiosity, and willing to take risks. All these facets
of the adolescent personality had positive benefits in the days
when he had to make the daunting leap from his sheltered life
as a child to face the challenges of a hard and demanding
adulthood, but what use can he put them to now? For the
teenager stuck largely in the world of the child, the character
traits that enabled him to tackle the challenges of growing up
now make him awkward, argumentative, demanding, difficult,
self-absorbed. The onset of a child's adolescence is no longer a
cause for celebration, but for commiseration between parents.
'Teenager now, is she? Cheer up, it won't last for ever!' We
roll our eyes, sigh, and sympathize with one another. Being the
parent of a teenager is hard.

We sometimes forget that it isn't an easy time for the
adolescent, either. The age of majority is set legally at 18, but
the young person ceases to be a child many years before that;
even the law acknowledges this to some extent, and children
gradually assume legal rights and responsibilities from a much
earlier age. Here is a sample of what the law allows young
people to do:

At 5 years
• Drink alcohol on private premises.

At 10 years
• Be fingerprinted, photographed and searched in police
custody, and charged with a crime.

At 12 years
• Buy a pet without a parent being present.

At 13 years
- Do certain jobs as specified in local by-laws (e.g. paper round).

At 14 years
- Enter licensed premises not covered by a children's licence (18 years in Northern Ireland).
- Enter into a credit or hire purchase agreement if an adult acts as guarantor.
- Hire a horse for riding without supervision.
- Be legally responsible for wearing a seat belt when a passenger in a car.

At 16 years
- Buy tobacco, cigarettes and cigarette papers (it is legal to smoke at any age).
- Buy or drink wine, beer, cider or perry with a meal in a hotel or restaurant, or in part of a pub that is set apart for eating meals.
- Choose and register with their own GP, and get confidential advice and treatment.
- Leave full-time education.
- Work full time, with restrictions (e.g. no bar work).
- Be charged with a criminal offence if they wilfully assault, ill treat or abandon a child left in their care.
- Marry in a register office, with parental consent.
- Marry in a church without parental consent, if the vicar agrees.
- Give consent to heterosexual intercourse.
- Leave home voluntarily.
- Buy public lottery tickets.
- Fly a glider.

At 17 years
- Drive a car or motorbike.
- Hold a private pilot's licence.

At 18 years
- Buy and drink any alcoholic beverage in a pub.
- Donate body and organs on death without parental consent.
- Buy solvents legally.
- Earn the National Minimum Wage.
- Marry without parental consent.
- Give consent to male homosexual intercourse.

The 13-year-old, then, is only three years away from being able to marry; the 16-year-old can leave home, get a job and fly a glider. Most teenagers are physically capable of becoming parents, yet society, school and family may treat them largely as children. What makes all this even harder for both them and their parents is that although they yearn to become independent, they will also continue to need the acceptance, love and support of their family for many years to come. Inevitably, frustrations, resentment and confusion arise for teenagers and their parents, and family life can become a battleground.

This book is for the parents and carers of teenagers. It will not provide easy answers to the difficult questions that parenting a young adult raises, but in it I have sought to explore the experience of being a teenager, the impact of teenage upheaval on the family, and ways in which communication between parent and adolescent child can be maintained and enhanced. I have also included some tried-and-tested practical measures for keeping teenagers safe and healthy, helping them to make the most of their education, and encouraging their development towards independence.

Although there will always be some conflict – and should be, as children strive to establish their own identity through differentiating themselves from their parents – an understanding of the processes involved, and a little forethought and planning, will help families to weather the storms, and to emerge from these often awkward (and sometimes downright frightening) teenage years with friendship and mutual trust intact.

1

Puberty and Adolescence

Puberty is the stage of development when sexual maturity begins and the reproductive organs become capable of functioning. This process usually starts between the ages of ten and fourteen, and may take anything from two to four years to complete.

The term 'adolescence' is broader, covering the whole period of transition from child to fully mature adult, so that while a boy or girl may be capable of becoming a parent at 14 or 15 (or considerably younger), he or she will remain an adolescent until mental and emotional development catches up with the purely physical changes – perhaps at the age of legal majority, or even later. For the purposes of this book, however, I will use the terms 'adolescent' and 'teenager' to describe young people who have entered puberty, but are not yet adults.

What happens to a child's body and mind during adolescence? The physical changes are often what we notice first. Some, but not all, depend on the gender of the developing child.

Girls

For most girls, puberty starts between the ages of 10 and 14, with the average age at which girls start their periods being at around 13. At 15 or 16, most girls are almost physically mature, and very close to their adult height. The first physical signs that puberty has begun include:

- The composition of sweat changes, and body odour becomes noticeable.
- Pubic and underarm hair starts to appear.
- Weight increases and body shape changes.
- Height increases.
- Breasts start to develop.

Alongside these visible changes, there are others that are not so easily observed – the internal and external sex organs grow in size, periods start, and the ovaries begin to produce eggs.

Weight and height

During puberty, a girl's body shape changes from the slim, straight figure of a child to the curved shape of a mature woman. Part of this process is a gain in weight, some of which is deposited as fat on the breasts, buttocks and hips. Girls may become slightly chubby during puberty, and this can be a source of anxiety to them, especially if it attracts teasing from their peers, who may not be developing at the same rate. This insecurity can contribute to the development of eating disorders (see Chapter 6).

Height increases rapidly, too, so that by 15 or 16 many girls have reached their full adult height. This, coupled with their now womanly figure, can make it very hard to guess their real age.

Breasts

During the general growth spurt of puberty, girls' breasts start to develop. First the nipple and areola (the dark area around the nipple) darken in colour, then the breast beneath starts to get bigger as its glandular tissue grows, and fat is deposited around it. Their developing breasts can be a source of embarrassment to adolescent girls, and some will adopt a characteristic, round-shouldered stoop in an unconscious effort to disguise them. Sometimes one breast grows faster than the other, and it is normal, even when they are fully developed, for breasts to be of different sizes. A bra is not necessary for breast health, but girls whose breasts are well developed may feel more comfortable wearing one, if only for sports. Sometimes growing breasts itch or tingle; this is quite normal, and will stop when breast growth is complete.

Voice

Although a girl's voice will not 'break' during puberty like a boy's, it will 'sweeten', becoming deeper and fuller in tone.

2

Menstruation

The average age for the onset of menstruation is around 13, and most girls will have their first period between 11 and 14. Some girls, though, may be as young as 8, while others may be 17 before they begin to menstruate. Once a girl has started her periods, she is ovulating, and therefore capable of becoming pregnant if she has unprotected sexual intercourse.

Before their first period starts, most girls will experience a slight vaginal discharge for a time, which will leave a white deposit on their knickers. This is nothing to worry about, but if the discharge smells unpleasant, has a greenish colour, or is associated with soreness or pain, it may be a sign of infection that needs treatment.

At first, periods are often irregular, settling into a regular cycle over a year or more. The average cycle, once established, is 28 days (from the start of one period to the start of the next), but individual cycles can vary considerably in length. Cramping pain is quite commonly associated with early periods, but if it is severe and persists, it is worth consulting a doctor or complementary health practitioner. As well as period pains, some girls may experience skin problems, mood swings, breast tenderness and bloating associated with periods, and these too can respond to conventional or complementary medical treatment.

Toxic Shock Syndrome

It is vital that young girls understand the importance of changing their tampons regularly, even if their blood loss is small, and use a towel rather than a tampon overnight. There is a danger of developing Toxic Shock Syndrome (TSS) if a tampon is worn for more than a few hours; TSS can be very serious, and a few women have died as a result.

Boys

On average, puberty starts later for boys, but for most is within the 10–14 age band. The first physical signs that a boy is entering puberty are:

- The sweat glands develop, and body odour becomes more noticeable.
- Pubic, body and facial hair starts to appear.
- The penis grows longer and thicker, and the testicles increase in size.
- Body weight and height increase rapidly.
- Erections become more frequent.

Less obviously, the testicles start to produce sperm.

Sexual organs

Early in puberty, the penis, scrotum and testicles begin to grow until they reach adult size. The rest of the body may grow more slowly, and the sexual organs may look out of proportion for a time, but sooner or later growth will balance out.

As well as growing, the sexual organs start to function in a sexual way. Boys will experience erections more frequently, and may have nocturnal emissions or 'wet dreams'. Spontaneous erections may become an embarrassment, although they are not nearly as noticeable as they feel. Pubic hair will grow at the base of the penis and around the testicles. Once the testicles are producing sperm, the adolescent boy is capable of getting a girl pregnant if he has unprotected sex with her.

Some boys notice changes in their breasts during puberty, with nipples becoming a little larger and darker and the breast tissue becoming more obvious. Sometimes these changes may be quite painful, and the boy who experiences them may worry that he's turning into a girl. In fact, they are a normal result of the hormonal activity surrounding puberty, and will settle down in time.

Height and weight

Puberty is a time of extremely fast growth for boys. They suddenly become much taller, and start to develop a more muscular physique with broader shoulders and a bigger chest. For some, this growth spurt is delayed, and although they usually catch up with their peers later, it can cause great anguish for a boy to remain, to all appearances, a child, while those around him are becoming men.

Although boys are slower to start their growth spurt, their rapid growth means that they may well overtake the girls; and boys' pubertal development will usually continue until they are at least 17. One of the noticeable effects of all this growth is on boys' appetites. They may seem to have 'hollow legs', eating far more than they did before the onset of puberty, and more than their sisters of the same age. Because of their rapid growth, too, boys of this age can be clumsy and gangly – not surprising when, during an intense growth spurt, a boy hardly seems to stay the same size for more than a day or two at a time. As growth slows, they will get used to their new size and regain the ease of movement and co-ordination they had before puberty began.

Voice

As puberty progresses, often over a considerable period but sometimes almost overnight, a boy's voice deepens, or 'breaks', from the high-pitched tones of childhood to the deeper voice of a man. Usually, this process starts at around 14 or 15, and is complete by the age of 17 or so, but can start later or take longer.

Shaving

A boy's facial hair growth usually starts with a light down on his upper lip and chin. At first he won't need to shave often – perhaps once a week or so – but the growth will thicken gradually until he is physically mature, when he will probably need to shave daily. Facial and chest hair are often among the last developments of puberty, so there is no need to worry if their appearance seems delayed.

Other physical changes in both boys and girls

Some of the changes of puberty are common to both sexes. For both boys and girls, growth during puberty is uneven – the skeleton grows first, and then the muscles develop to fit the bone structure. Because of this, adolescents will go through long periods when their bodies simply cannot do things they did

5

easily before puberty began. They may be clumsy and awkward, lack the muscular strength to control their new, lanky frame, and lose the physical skills and sporting prowess they established as a child. This can be profoundly worrying and depressing for adolescents, particularly if others pick on their deficiencies or tell them that they are not trying hard enough. It is very important they understand that this is just a phase that they will pass through in time.

Skin

Everyone has spots occasionally, but teenagers get them more often than most, due largely to the effects of the hormone surges of puberty on oil secretions in their skin. For many, simple self-help measures will keep the problem under control, but serious spots can become infected, leading to acne (see Chapter 6).

Sweat and body odour

During puberty the sweat glands develop and the composition of sweat changes to contain a powerful sexual attractant. The action of bacteria on this substance, however, produces the characteristic and unpleasant smell we think of as 'body odour', and this can become evident in children as young as ten. Fresh sweat does not smell unpleasant, and washing and regular changing of clothes, along with the use of an underarm deodorant, will keep body odour at bay. Vaginal deodorants, however, should not be necessary for girls and may cause irritation.

Sleep

One of the effects of the physical change and growth of puberty is the need for more sleep. The answer is not, unfortunately, simply to send your teenager to bed earlier – another effect of puberty is a shift from child to adult sleep patterns.

Regardless of when we go to bed, our ability to fall asleep is governed by the release in our bodies of serotonin. In children, this takes place at around seven o'clock in the evening. In adults, serotonin is released at around ten o'clock, and once this adult pattern has kicked in, it will be difficult for the teenager to get to sleep much before this time. The result is often that adolescents who have to get up early for school are still tired and difficult to wake, may not eat a proper breakfast, and may spend the early part of the school day fighting off the urge to sleep.

Early puberty

Although most children enter puberty between the ages of 10 and 14, a few will start much earlier. One recent study found that as many as one in six of the girls studied showed signs of puberty by eight years old, and that one in fourteen boys of the same age had pubic hair. One possible explanation of this apparent shift of puberty down the age scale is that birth weights have risen over the 30 years or so since earlier studies; and it is known that the onset of sexual maturity is linked to body weight. Rarely, very early puberty can indicate some underlying health problem, so it is worth talking to your doctor if your child develops years ahead of his or her classmates. Generally, though, problems associated with early puberty are more likely to result from the psychological effects of being far out of step developmentally with friends and classmates.

Delayed puberty

The timing and duration of puberty is genetically determined, so parents who have been late developers themselves are likely to have children with the same tendencies. They can help their child come to terms with what can be a worrying and humiliating situation by sharing their own experiences, and pointing out that it all worked out in the end. If early signs of puberty have not appeared by the age of 14, however, in either sex, it is worth seeking advice from the family doctor. Puberty that begins, but is not complete after five years (i.e. periods fail to start, voice unbroken), also requires investigation. In girls, the cessation or non-appearance of periods can be caused by an eating disorder (see Chapter 6).

The mental and emotional effects of puberty

The physical changes of puberty have far-reaching effects on the mind and emotions of the adolescent. At no other time in our lives (with the possible exception of pregnancy) do our bodies change so much in such a short space of time. The hormones that flood the adolescent body expose the teenager to powerful, new feelings, emotions and drives, causing profound mood swings from elation and energy to depression and self-doubt. Parents may forget, in their struggle to cope with what appears at times to be a rather unlikeable stranger, that their teenager too is discovering new aspects of his personality every day and is often at a loss to predict or understand his own emotions. If we think back to our own adolescence, though, we may remember what preoccupied our own teenage selves:

Body image

Most teenagers don't like the way they look. They compare themselves endlessly with their peers and the icons they are offered in the media, and may feel that they can never measure up. Both girls and boys may become very concerned about their weight, particularly as they pass through the 'puppy fat' phase of puberty, and this may lead them to try to lose weight by restricting their diet. As already mentioned, some children will succumb to eating disorders (see Chapter 6).

Their rapidly changing bodies may make teenagers feel clumsy and awkward (see above), and they may feel that they will be stuck in this clumsy phase for ever. Even worse, their bodies may suddenly let them down. Spots may erupt just when they most want to make a good impression, and spontaneous erections and leaking menstrual blood threaten embarrassment. For boys, the breaking voice may be so unpredictable that they daren't speak in public, and insecurity and lack of confidence are often the result.

Relationships with peers

The focus of a teenager's life shifts at puberty from family and home to friends, and it is to friends, rather than parents, that teenagers instinctively turn when they are worried or unhappy. This can feel like rejection to parents, but it is simply part of the teenager's need to establish his own identity and gain independence.

Acceptance by their peer group becomes overwhelmingly important and, in order to achieve this, adolescents will strive to conform in every detail to the prevailing norm. Because 'fitting in' is so important, any physical development that takes place early or late, putting teenagers out of step with their classmates, may make them really miserable.

Adolescent insecurities and the overriding need to fit in make teenagers particularly easy targets for bullying. Rejection by peers is particularly painful during adolescence, and there have been tragic instances of children taking their own lives because of persistent bullying (see Chapter 5 for further information).

Relationship with parents

Being a teenager may be hell, but it's a difficult time for parents too. During the early period of rapid change and growth, you may sometimes feel as though you are sharing your home with a stranger who is shifting constantly between adult and child. Suddenly, your child questions your views on everything, and argues his own, with often shockingly different opinions. It almost seems as if he is making a point of adopting beliefs that contradict your own, and of course to some extent he is – in the struggle to establish their own identity, teenagers need to differentiate and distance themselves from their parents and find space in which to grow into themselves.

Part of the teenager's efforts to establish independence from parents may involve rejecting some of their values and expectations. Also, teenagers will often respond to questions, comments or actions with sarcasm and rudeness, and this can make parents feel hurt and angry, and some conflict is almost inevitable. In Chapter 9 we will look at ways of handling such conflict constructively – or at least limiting the damage to family relationships – but it is important to remember that the family provides a safe environment in which the adolescent can learn to deal with his own emotions and the feelings of others without permanently damaging them, or his relationship with them. What he learns through these conflicts at home will help him to make and maintain successful, fulfilling relationships in adult life.

The adolescent brain

It isn't only inexperience that makes our children vulnerable. Though physical maturity may come early for some, the adolescent brain differs physiologically from that of an adult; while adults use the frontal lobe to rationalize and modify emotional responses to situations and events, the young teenager is only just starting to develop this ability. Because of this, adolescents are less able than adults to assess the possible consequences of their actions, and more likely to react instinctively. This tendency can lead them to take risks, and treat others in ways that seem insensitive and needlessly confrontational. Throughout adolescence, they need the example and advice of parents and others to show them how to behave in adult ways, but it is not easy for them to accept that need in themselves – the great challenge to all those involved in caring for or educating teenagers is to provide the help and protection they need in a way that they can accept.

The danger is that, in his efforts to separate himself from his family, the teenager might break his links with his source of security and support. The teenage years are fraught with challenge and insecurity, and it will be a long time before the adolescent ceases to need the family safety net to fall back on. Simply caving in to all your adolescent's demands and tantrums in order to avoid conflict is not the answer – this conflict is a natural and essential part of his growing up and differentiating himself from his parents, and often the adolescent who pushes against his parents and meets no resistance will simply push harder and harder in an effort to find a point at which the necessary separation can occur. This can lead to more and more extreme behaviour, which causes anxiety and distress to both teenager and parents, and may eventually cause their relationship to break down altogether.

Keeping a sense of proportion

The teenage years can be a time of great stress for parents, but it is important to remember that there is an end to it. The result of successful parenting is an independent, mature individual who can think for herself and determine the course of her own life. In order to achieve this maturity and independence, your child needs to step away from the parent/child relationship, returning as an adult relating to other adults.

2

Communication

Conversation with teenagers can sometimes seem impossible. Whatever you say meets with a sullen or argumentative response, your opinions are rejected out of hand, and your attempts to share and help with your child's problems are rebuffed ungraciously. At other times, you can converse with your teenager as though he were another adult.

How can we make communication easier for all concerned, and avoid outright conflict over apparently trivial issues? Here are some simple basic rules of communication that work in all relationships, whether with child, adolescent or adult. They will not always make conversation with your teenager easy and straightforward, but they will often help. Even when he is at his least co-operative your child will learn, by example, communication skills that will prove essential in his adult family, social and work relationships.

Respect

One of the most frequently criticized aspects of adolescent behaviour is the lack of respect they show to others, and especially to their parents. One of the more trying manifestations of this is the appearance of sarcasm and heavy-handed, mocking humour in the teenager's conversational repertoire.

Teenagers are in the process of becoming adults; they know that they cannot relate to their parents for ever in the way they did during their childhood, and they must find new ways of interacting with their family and the people they meet in the wider world. In families where parents treat their children and each other with respect, the maturing adolescent will have a positive model of adult behaviour to base his developing attitudes upon. Although, as he comes to see his parents as normal, fallible people, he may show his disappointment and disillusionment by offhand or downright rude behaviour, he will eventually settle into an adult pattern of interaction with his family. This becomes much more difficult if his parents, in struggling to cope with his disrespectful behaviour, begin to behave like teenagers themselves, and respond with insults of their own, or insist on continuing to treat him as a child.

Difficult though it can sometimes be when they still behave childishly at times, it is important to try to speak to teenagers as young adults rather than as children. Showing that you trust and respect them by giving them responsibility will help, and many gain enormously in confidence when they get their first paid work or are asked for their opinion in major family decisions. It is a good rule of thumb always to make it clear that you are confident in your child's ability to do the right thing in any given situation, even though he will not always achieve this. Where the worst is expected of them, adolescents will, more often than not, live down to expectations.

Listening

Often, and especially when there is conflict within the family, we are so concerned with getting our point across that we forget to listen to what the others involved in the conversation are saying. Communication is a two-way street, and the first step to making it effective is to listen. It isn't enough, either, just to hear what is said – we must also make clear to the other party that we have heard and understood their point of view, and given it due consideration. We can do this by:

- Listening, without interruption, to what they have to say.
- Asking for clarification of any part we don't understand.
- 'Playing back' to the other party our understanding of what they have said.
- Answering the points they have raised.

Having done these things, we are entitled to ask that they do the same.

While it is often difficult to hear your adolescent expound

what you feel is a ridiculous or dangerous point of view, rubbishing or laughing at her opinions will simply serve to entrench her in a position that she may only have taken up experimentally; teenagers will often 'try out' different points of view until they find one that 'fits'. Far more will be achieved by a reasoned discussion, even if it appears at the time that you are the only one being reasonable.

Acknowledging feelings

Feelings can be a difficult area. What seems trivial to you can be overwhelmingly important to your teenager, so that small events, like falling out with a best friend, can cause dreadful misery. Saying 'It's silly to feel like this – it's just not that important' will not help; to be truly supportive you must first recognize and acknowledge your child's feelings as real, even though your own reaction to the situation might be different. Janice's memories of her own adolescence helped her to understand her daughter's point of view:

> I found it hard to deal with my daughter's horrified protests at being asked to take responsibility for very minor household chores – then I remembered my own reaction to being asked by my mother to put dirty dishes into the dishwasher, rather than simply leaving them lying around on the kitchen table. I couldn't believe she could be so mean – this wasn't my job; there I was, up to my eyes in homework, out all day at school and with only the evenings to do important things like phoning friends, listening to music and experimenting with hair and make-up, and she'd suddenly decided to lumber me with household chores that I had never been expected to do before. Where would it all end? It seemed perfectly reasonable to me then that I should feel outraged and put upon, although it embarrasses me to remember it now.

It is up to us as parents to accept our teenager's feelings, to explain, and go on explaining, that along with the privileges of increasing maturity go responsibilities – and to weather the storm of our children's outrage in the knowledge that they will eventually come to see things in a more adult way.

Agreeing to disagree

During their teenage years, children begin to form their own opinions on all sorts of things, some of them issues on which parents feel that the family as a whole already has an established and shared point of view. It can be very difficult to hear your child questioning the attitudes and opinions that form the cornerstones of your way of life, and exasperating to hear them advocate change without apparently understanding all the issues involved.

Life can look very black and white to teenagers as they develop a new moral and ideological outlook and try to find their place in the scheme of things, and they will often wholeheartedly embrace causes that they feel are important. Your child may become vegetarian, espouse far left- or right-wing politics or reject your family's religion; she may feel that war is wrong, whatever the cause, and say so to members of the family who have taken part in armed conflicts for what they believe were good reasons. Discussion of her views and of the issues involved is fine, but there may come a point where you have to agree to disagree on this particular subject, acknowledging her point of view even though you don't share it.

Bear in mind that these may not be the views she holds for the rest of her life; they are her first stabs at making sense of a complex world, and experience will almost certainly broaden her understanding of the issues involved and modify her opinions – as it may yours.

Agreeing to disagree about the principles behind your child's behaviour doesn't mean that the behaviour itself can't change. Where your adolescent's behaviour is causing distress or harm to herself or others, it may be necessary to acknowledge that she has a right to her principles, but not to foist the consequences on others. While you are still legally and morally responsible for her, you have a duty to see that she doesn't break the law or do herself or others harm.

Be positive

Don't talk to your child only when there are problems. Tell him often how pleased and proud you are of his achievements, how much you like him, how good he looks today. Thank him for any help he gives you, however little and late it may be. Without this positive reinforcement, communicating with you can soon become a thing to be avoided at all costs, and for him there can seem little point in trying to please you if his efforts are never noticed.

Privacy, lying and secrecy

As your child's body starts to change and he begins to experience new thoughts and feelings, it is natural that he will become more self-conscious than he was as a child. There is much that he has yet to make sense of himself, and he doesn't want to share everything that is happening in his life with his family. He is more likely, in fact, to talk to his friends about things that are really important to him – after all, they are going through the same changes and are far more likely to recognize and understand his feelings without criticism or expectations.

It is still important for parents to show an interest in what their teenage children are doing, both in and out of school, but not to the point of prying into their personal lives. Issues of privacy often come to a head where teenagers' bedrooms are concerned. Both boys and girls need to feel that they have some personal space in which they can escape from the family and simply be themselves, and teenagers' rooms often become intense expressions of their occupants' personality, with every square centimetre of available wall space covered in posters, and shelves and cupboards loaded with possessions whose sole purpose is to make a statement about the interests and obsessions of the adolescent and his peer group. It is not uncommon for teenagers to carry this statement of individuality to the point of extreme untidiness, and this is where conflict can often arise.

If this is to be truly the adolescent's own space, then we really have no right as parents to dictate how it should look. If there are clothes strewn ankle-deep over the floor or piles of magazines on every surface, and your child likes it like that, there is no real reason to expect him to change things to suit your preferences. In practice, however, it is very hard for a houseproud parent to accept that their child might want to live not just in disorder, but in squalor, and it may be necessary to have some basic expectations that are understood and agreed by all concerned:

Hygiene

When untidiness becomes unpleasant for the whole family or is a health hazard, it ceases to be an acceptable expression of individuality. It is reasonable to expect your child to dispose of dirty cups and plates and half-eaten food in the appropriate places, and not to leave them under the bed until they grow multi-coloured mould and smell abominable.

Convenience

Your child should bear the consequences of her chosen lifestyle, not you. Clothes that need washing should be deposited in the washing basket at least two days (or whatever is practical in your household) before they are needed, and anything that isn't will not be washed; similarly, you should not be expected to search for or replace belongings lost in the debris on the bedroom floor. Also, other people's or general family property should not be removed to the teenager's room and left there.

Tidying

Sometimes teenagers' rooms get so bad that even they are depressed by the mess, but they are so daunted by the task of sorting everything out that they don't know where to start. In this case, they may need help with sorting through their belongings and finding places to store everything they want to keep. Orderliness is a skill that it takes time to learn, and helping your child to straighten up her room will help her to develop this ability. Often a teenager will be better motivated to keep tidy a room that she has planned and decorated herself than one that has been imposed on her, and it is worth allowing a colour scheme that makes your eyes water to provide a space that your child feels is really her own, and wants to maintain.

If things get to the point where you feel that you must tidy the room yourself, give your child fair warning, so that he can put away anything secret or embarrassing. Telling your child that if he doesn't tidy his room over the next weekend you will do it yourself may be enough to motivate him to get started – if only to prevent you rooting about among his personal possessions.

Lying and secrecy

There are bound to be things that your teenager doesn't want you to know. Often, these will be small secrets, like which boy she fancies or the fact he's got a couple of girlie magazines under his bed. We really don't need to know these things, and it is best to acknowledge that and not to question teenagers on these unimportant issues. There is a danger that, if we probe too deeply into every aspect of their lives, our adolescents will be forced to preserve their privacy by lying to us; this is a precedent it would be unwise to establish if we want our children to come to us for help with the really important issues in their lives.

Hugs and kisses

As children pass through puberty and become sexually mature, they may begin to shy away from the physical gestures of affection – hugs, kisses and cuddles – that they accepted and enjoyed as children. This is part of the natural process of distancing themselves from their parents, but it would be a mistake to feel you should never cuddle your son or daughter again. Be guided by your adolescent – while a goodbye kiss at the school gate may be out of the question after the age of nine or ten, even the 15-year-old who towers over his mum needs a hug now and again in the privacy of his own home.

It may be less appropriate for other, more distant family members and friends to be physically affectionate towards your sexually maturing child. It is very important that children, from an early age, understand that their body is their own and that they have the right to repel unwanted physical advances – this knowledge will protect them to some extent from physical and sexual abuse by both known adults and strangers, and is important when it comes to the avoidance of risky behaviour like drug and alcohol use, and unsafe sex, later on in adolescence.

No child should be forced or persuaded to have close physical contact with an adult – whether it is a kiss on the cheek or a cuddle on the lap – and young teenage girls in particular may need to have it pointed out to them that it is no longer appropriate for adult males to tickle or fondle them as they did when they were children.

Lone parenting

Communicating with a teenager is difficult enough at times, but what happens if you are the single parent of a child of the opposite sex? In practice, this may not be as much of a problem as some parents fear; although in an ideal world there would always be a same-sex parent available and willing to help each child through the difficulties of maturing into an adult, this is often not the case even in two-parent families. A sympathetic, concerned parent who is willing to research and provide appropriate information will do a good job of supporting his or her child, regardless of gender – and probably much better than an uninterested or unimaginative parent of the same sex could.

What adolescents in a single-parent family may lack is an adult who can say simply, 'I know how you feel. I felt like that too.' They will get this support, to some extent, from friends, but other teenagers cannot put the ups and downs of adolescence in the perspective of adult experience. Older siblings, relatives, friends, teachers and even written accounts of adolescence in books and magazines can often fill the gap and provide a positive role model that will help the adolescent towards an understanding of what being an adult man or woman is really all about.

The imperfect parent

One of the difficult things for many parents to accept is that, along with questioning their values, their adolescent starts to see them as whole people, warts and all, and to judge them against other adults. Gone are the days when he looked up to his parents as all-knowing, all-powerful, almost godlike figures. Now he will notice, and point out with painful honestly and regularity, all the little weaknesses, defects and inconsistencies that his parents recognize in themselves, and quite a few that hadn't occurred to them. This is not a pleasant experience, and can arouse feelings of hostility and competition in parents, straining family relationships to breaking point. This phase won't last for ever, and there are some tips for dealing with it:

- Don't jump on the bandwagon. Tempting though it may be to join in when your child points out one of the most trying aspects of your partner's personality, it helps no one to have members of the family 'ganging up' against one another.
- Don't get into a slanging match with your child. Trading insult for insult will only escalate the situation, and the battle is not an equal one. Although your child appears to be sure enough of himself to challenge you on all sorts of issues, your opinion of him is still central to his personality and an insensitive remark from you can hurt him deeply and permanently.
- Talk to friends and relatives who also have teenagers – sharing your experiences will help to put them in perspective, and you can share tips for coping.

- Give yourself a break. Parenting is hard, demanding work, and you won't be able to keep it up if you don't allow yourself time to do some things just for yourself.
- If you feel things are getting out of hand, don't be afraid to ask for help. See Useful Addresses at the back of this book for groups and agencies offering support for families with teenagers.

It is the job of a parent to absorb a good deal of rejection and be unharmed by it, and not to return it in kind. Do your best to remain reasonable, even when your teenager tries to raise the temperature of the debate. If it gets out of hand and you feel unable to cope in a restrained way, simply end it by walking away, and returning to the discussion when tempers have cooled.

3
Conformity and Freedom

One of the things that can make parents suddenly and forcibly aware of their child's inexorable progress towards independence is the realization that he doesn't even want to *look* like one of the family any more, and this can be surprisingly distressing. We are so used to seeing our family as a unit in the face of the outside world that it can feel almost like a betrayal when one of us adopts modes of dress and behaviour that identify that person with a different group. We can find this profoundly worrying without really knowing why, and a good deal of conflict can result.

The teenager's desperate need to conform with his peer group in every possible way is nowhere more clearly expressed than through his clothing. This need, coupled with his increasing preoccupation with his own body image, means that the teenager's idea of what is and is not acceptable becomes so specific that it is almost impossible for parents to buy clothing for him in his absence and to get it right. All this can make life very difficult, and sometimes very expensive, for parents – especially when he swears that everyone at school has £80 trainers except him, and that he will be a social outcast if he is seen wearing the almost identical £30 ones they favour. Although he may be exaggerating the number of parents who really are willing to shell out a small fortune to keep their child at the cutting edge of fashion, he may well have a point about his likely excommunication if he turns up at school wearing something that is deemed unacceptable – teenagers can be ruthless in their rejection of anyone who does not conform scrupulously to their unwritten rules of appearance and behaviour.

In the course of finding out who they really are, and especially in the early teenage years, adolescents will experiment with a range of different looks. It can be very difficult to see children making dreadful fashion mistakes and not to say anything, but the teenager's body image is often so tenuous that even the slightest criticism may shake their confidence to its foundations. If you have to comment, try to be positive: 'I thought the longer one looked *really* good on you.'

Although there may be some bizarre short-term consequences, this period of experimentation will eventually result in your teenager settling on a 'look', often defined by the group he identifies with – sporty, fashionable, or one of any number of other possible variations.

Most schools will specify a uniform which, although teenagers bitterly resent wearing it, simplifies matters enormously by setting limits within which clothing for school must be chosen. Outside school, though, how can you prevent your child from making a fool of herself – and embarrassing you – by appearing in public bizarrely dressed? You can't – not all of the time, anyway – and most of the time it isn't very important anyway. For the rare occasions when it really matters, a family wedding or a job interview for example, most teenagers will be willing to conform to an acceptable standard of dress, as long as their everyday clothing is a matter for their own choice.

If conflict over clothing arises, be prepared to ask yourself whether it really matters if your son turns up, for instance, at the office 'fathers and sons' day in cricket whites, a borrowed jacket, and a shirt whose collar won't fasten underneath his badly knotted tie. After all, everyone he meets there will have been young once, and some will have teenagers of their own.

Hair

Like clothing, hairstyle can be a badge of allegiance, clearly stating which group a teenager identifies with. Hair soon grows again, colours fade or grow out, and although you may feel that your adolescent's hairstyle does nothing for him, there seems little reason to oppose any but the wildest excess if he has set his heart on it. His school, though, may have other ideas.

While school uniform or dress code are usually covered by a written policy, matters of personal appearance such as hairstyle and body-piercing (see Chapter 6) are rarely covered in detail.

Occasionally the whole issue of personal appearance becomes a battleground, often between parents and school – with the child stuck somewhere in the middle, and there have been a few well-publicized cases of head teachers suspending pupils because of what they consider unsuitable haircuts.

Common sense usually prevails in the end – where a hairstyle does not look unduly unkempt, or impair a child's ability to learn, it would be hard for a head teacher to justify suspending a pupil on the grounds of taste alone – but it is regrettable that the child's education has been interrupted and his relationship with the school soured. If your child is considering a change of style, it is worth anticipating problems and avoiding confrontation as far as possible, even if you think that the rules are somewhat arbitrary. If your teenager wants to look different, try the following suggestions:

- Dye hair unusual colours over the summer holidays, with semi-permanent dye that will wash out before the autumn term starts.
- Choose a haircut that can be rendered fairly normal-looking for school, either by tying up or gelling down.

Body-piercing

There has been a great upsurge in the popularity of body-piercing in recent years, particularly among the young. The part of the body to be pierced, commonly the ear, nose, lip, tongue or navel, but sometimes other areas including the genitals, is cleaned with a sterilizing solution, and pierced with a sharp instrument. A metal stud or ring is inserted and the area gradually heals round it. The 'sleeper' inserted when the piercing is carried out can then be replaced with a great variety of commercially available ornamental studs, hoops and pins.

The danger of body-piercing is the procedure itself: serious bleeding can occur, particularly in the case of the tongue; nerves and muscles can be damaged during piercing, leading to pain or paralysis; and there is a danger of infection if the wound is not kept clean, or if the equipment used was not effectively sterilized. It is also possible for the HIV virus to be transmitted via instruments used in piercing, although this is fairly unlikely in practice.

Anyone can legally carry out piercings, although premises used for commercial piercing are subject to inspection and licensing by the local environmental health department. There are no legal restrictions on the age at which you can have your ears or other body parts pierced, but some piercers will not carry out the procedure on children or teenagers without parental consent.

Although professional piercing is largely unregulated, the Association of Professional Piercers runs a voluntary register of piercers, and can provide information about its members (see Useful Addresses at the back of this book).

Tattooing

While changes of image – e.g. clothing, hair and body-piercing – can all be undone, tattooing is designed to last. Although tattoo removal by laser or surgery is possible, it can be expensive and the results are variable, often leaving permanent scarring. An increasing number of large organizations will not employ people with tattoos, and one consultant dealing with tattoo removal reports that he sees two or three people a year who have attempted suicide because of their tattoos.

It is illegal for a tattoo artist, who must be licensed, to tattoo anyone under 18, and he must conform to strict hygiene regulations to prevent the transmission of disease via his equipment. If your teenager is contemplating a tattoo, it is worth pointing out to him that it could prevent him from getting the job he wants later in life, and that he might find it a social embarrassment in a few years' time; after all, he is not likely to be wearing the same clothes or hairstyle 20 or 30 years hence – why should he expect that he will still be happy with the same tattoo? Temporary tattoos that can be applied for a special occasion and then washed off for school or work are now widely available, and anyone who is considering the permanent variety would be well advised to try a temporary one for a time before they commit themselves.

Conformity

Issues of personal liberty can arouse very strong feelings in both children and parents, but it is worth remembering that very few of us are free to look or behave exactly as we wish all the time. Whether it is wearing uniform for school or designer-distressed jeans for a party, we are all conforming to the requirements of one group or another.

That said, it is not realistic for parents to expect their offspring to conform to their standards of dress and behaviour in all areas – indeed, it would be worrying if any teenager were happy simply to become a clone of her parents. What makes us able to achieve in life, gives us the strength to hold beliefs and stick to principles, and to interact and form satisfying and lasting relationships with others, is our sense of our own identity – what makes us different from everyone else in the world. There are situations in which we hope our children would not conform to peer group pressures – and bullying, drug taking and petty crime must be high on this list. A child who has a clear sense of his own identity and worth is much better able to resist these pressures than one who has been brought up to accept others' views of life unquestioningly.

It may be inconvenient, and sometimes maddening and worrying, but it is healthy and right that children should question the values of their parents and of the wider society in which they live, and through this process they will eventually arrive at a set of principles of their own that will sustain them through life. If we don't want our children to reject everything that we have learned – often through painful trial and error – in our own lives, we need to be very clear in our own minds about which issues are really important and which ones are simply to do with keeping up appearances or avoiding embarrassment.

Responsibility

One of the things we have to accept about our growing teenagers is that no longer can we *make* them do what we want. If it comes to out-and-out conflict, ultimately the teenager can simply refuse to do what his parents ask – tidy his room, cut his hair, be back in the house before midnight – and there is precious little that they can do about it. Unless we propose to lock them in their rooms and never allow them out of the house unaccompanied, we must rely on their co-operation in keeping to any rules and standards of behaviour we may set for and with them, and that co-operation will be founded on their sense of responsibility – the conviction that what they do has consequences that will matter to them and to other people who are important to them.

There can be no responsibility without choice, and decision-making is a skill like any other; it takes time to learn, and practice is essential. The adolescent who has not had the opportunity to make choices throughout childhood, from bedroom decor to after-school activity, will be faced, quite unprepared, with major, life-changing choices concerning alcohol, tobacco and drug use, sexual involvement, money matters, and a host of other issues – and his parents will not be around to help him make them. These are areas where mistakes can have far-reaching consequences, and not safe territory for his first, faltering steps in self-determination.

We get so used to making decisions for our children when they are young that it can be hard to know when to stop. With a bit of forethought and restraint, however, we can help even very young children to make choices, allowing them increasing opportunities to make their own decisions, and sometimes to discover the consequences of their own mistakes, as they grow older.

As children move into adolescence, choices arise that will impact seriously on their lives – choice of secondary school and of GCSE subjects, choice of friendships and out-of-school activities, and many more. Although the final say may sometimes have to remain with parents, the wishes and opinions of young people should always be sought and taken into account when decisions that affect their lives have to be made. Involvement in the decision-making process will provide the opportunity to learn about gathering, presenting and weighing evidence, assessing consequences, and arriving at a considered, balanced conclusion – all valuable life skills.

Dr Haim G. Ginott, a psychologist who worked extensively with children and parents in the 1960s, neatly summed up this most difficult aspect of parenting like this:

Education for responsibility can start very early in the child's life. Responsibility is fostered by allowing children a voice, and wherever indicated, a choice, in matters that affect them ... There are matters that fall entirely within the child's realm of responsibility. In such matters he should have his choice. There are matters affecting the child's welfare that are exclusively within our realm of responsibility. In such matters he may have a voice, but not a choice. We make the choice for him – while helping him to accept the inevitable. (Dr Haim G. Ginott, *Between Parent and Child*, Staples, 1969)

Dr Ginott goes on to describe situations in which children can be allowed choice, even though that choice may not be totally free. In the case of the young teenager, for example, this might mean saying, 'Here is a range of shoes I am willing to buy for you – which of them would you like?' or 'You are too young to stay at home while the rest of us go on holiday, but would you rather go to X or Y?' Much conflict with teenagers could be avoided if they felt that, while they do not always have a choice in decisions concerning themselves and their activities, they always have a voice, and one that will be listened to and seriously considered by their parents, teachers and others who have responsibility for them.

Although the adolescent needs to experience some responsibility in order to grow, she also needs to know that there are some things in life that it is not in her power to influence, for good or ill – her parents' personal happiness and their relationship with each other is one of these areas. Allowing or encouraging a teenager to feel that she can 'ruin your life', or that you 'couldn't manage without her', imposes a burden that she hasn't the maturity or emotional strength to carry. It isn't always easy to make this distinction between love and dependency, particularly when we are feeling emotionally starved in other areas of our lives, but good parenting requires that we protect our children from the consequences of our own problems wherever we can.

Parenting teenagers can put a great strain on marriages, for several reasons:

- Teenagers question everything, and this includes the inconsistencies in their parents' relationship that they have themselves avoided examining, sometimes for many years.
- The challenging behaviour of adolescents can cause disagreement between parents about who is to blame and how it should be handled.
- The constant presence and scrutiny of their teenage children can leave parents with little or no privacy in which to nurture their own relationship.

Despite all these pressures, it is important that parents present a consistent and united front when important issues are discussed and decisions made that affect their teenager. Unfortunately, even parents who have agreed on the upbringing of their younger children sometimes find it harder to reach a consensus when they become adolescent. There are several reasons for this, among them:

- Our own experiences as adolescents tend to influence the way we see our children at that age. For instance, the father who spent his youth bedding as many girls as he could may wish to impose stricter curfew restrictions on his teenage daughter than the mother whose early experience of sexual relationships was positive and safe.
- The expectations that our parents had of us as adolescents will affect our expectations of our own children. Where parents' experiences differ, disagreements may follow.

Many problems can be avoided if parents take the time together to talk over contentious issues before they discuss them with their teenager. Where conflict arises unexpectedly, it may be better to put off the discussion until you've had a chance to talk it over between yourselves.

When the pressures of parenting an adolescent seem over-whelming, it can help to remind yourself that your teenager is still 'under construction'. This can be a difficult time, but the upheaval in the child's life associated with the rapid development of puberty will eventually come to an end. It is not necessary to stamp on all the ups and downs of teenage behaviour lest they persist and become features of the adult that your child will become – in time he will mature, and the biggest danger is probably not that he will retain the behaviour of adolescence because you failed to stop him from doing so, but that he will be frozen in adolescence by his parents' inability to allow him to grow up and away from them. The most helpful and timely motto for any parent of teenage children may well, in fact, be – 'Don't panic!'

4

School

School isn't an easy place for many teenagers to be. Until relatively recently, adolescents spent their days working alongside their elders, learning about life as an adult from their example. Modern systems of education deprive children of both contact with adults and the opportunity to play an active and responsible part in the adult world. In return, they are offered a great range of knowledge, which may or may not contribute to their choice of employment and interests in the future.

Some welcome this opportunity to learn, and use it to work towards long-term goals. For a sizeable group of disaffected teenagers, however, school becomes a pointless and galling waste of time. Secondary schools make few allowances for the physical and emotional upheaval of puberty; teachers rarely get to know their pupils well enough to provide the supportive adult role models that they need, and the large groups of adolescents they teach are necessarily bound by often rigid and sometimes arbitrary rules that offend against their very strong sense of justice and fairness, and allow them little chance to take responsibility. The power that their teachers have over them may become a source of resentment and a challenge to misbehave, and school work a trial to be got out of the way as swiftly, and with as little effort, as possible.

The first real opportunity for the teenager to opt out of education completely comes at 16. Many feel they have grown out of school, and can't wait to leave. Faced with the chance to make their first big decision about their future, the short-term advantages of escaping school may feel far more pressing to the adolescent than the vague benefit of staying on for another two years in an environment that just doesn't seem to fit any more.

A similar crisis hits when the transition from school to university looms. After two years of intense pressure to achieve the A-level grades required, with three more years of exams ahead and the trauma of leaving home and adapting to a completely different way of life to face, some young people

31

may feel overwhelmed and opt out, though the gap year can sometimes provide a solution for this.

Some adolescents will already have a clear idea of what they want to do with their adult lives, and will be motivated by this to achieve whatever academic success they need for their chosen career. For a large proportion of teenagers, however, the future is less certain. They may be so busy rejecting the outlook of their parents' generation that they can't imagine ever wanting a conventional job, or so uncertain about who they are and what they want from life that they just can't see any clear path for the future. If this applies to your child, your overwhelming urge will be to convince him of the importance of his school career, but before you can do this you need to be very clear about your reasons for wanting him to succeed.

What's in it for you?

Our children represent the biggest investment of our lives, in terms of love, time and often money as well. Not only do we want the best for them, but what they achieve contributes to our feelings of success or failure as parents. This is perfectly understandable – parenting is a hard job to which we devote many years of our lives, and there is little recognition for it. We all want to be well thought of by others and to feel good about our own achievements, and our children's educational successes are often our only public proof that we have made a good job of it.

What's in it for your teenager?

Most parents would probably say they wanted their child to do well at school so that he could get a good and fulfilling job, and have a comfortable and successful life as an adult. For the teenager whose heart is set upon becoming a doctor or a lawyer, education is obviously crucial to achieving his ambitions. The days have gone, however, when a university degree assured its holder of a good job, or indeed any job at all, and many people still have satisfying and fulfilling careers without academic qualifications. For some teenagers, then, further years in full-time education after 16 or 18 may be of less long-term value than vocational training or even a full-time job.

If you want to provide your child with motivation to stay on, or simply to succeed, at school, and are sure that what you are proposing is really in his best interests, you will need to arm yourself with some examples of its benefits *to him*. Let's look at the reasons you might give your teenager for trying to do well at school:

- *Keeping his options open*
  It is important that your teenager understands that while he may see himself now as a self-employed website designer, or expect to take on the family business, circumstances may well change. If he wants to retrain at a later date, but hasn't got the basic qualifications to do so, it can be difficult, expensive and time-consuming to catch up, and you may not be able to support him financially while he does.
- *Changing his mind*
  He won't be wearing the same clothes or listening to the same music in 15 years' time, and he might not want to do the same job or have the same interests either. He may one day want to follow a different path, whether this means a change of job or a course of study, and a set of basic qualifications will enable him to do this.
- *Building self-esteem*
  Quite apart from the practical considerations, sticking at things and doing them well, even if we can't see any immediate benefit from them, go a long way towards making us feel good about ourselves, and building the confidence we need to tackle important challenges. How will he feel about himself if he gives up now?
- *Broadening his outlook on life*
  Education isn't just about work. Although some subjects appear to have little practical relevance (Religious Education or History, for example), they do help us to understand the world we live in and the people around us, and that brings all

sorts of very tangible benefits in our working and personal lives.

- *This is just a bad patch – you'll feel better about it later*
  When your child is going through a bad patch – particularly as exams approach, but also when things in his personal life aren't going too well – it can help to reassure him that you have felt just the same, and that he will feel much better once the immediate pressure has eased. Planning a holiday or outing for the future can help, as can providing a 'day off' at the time.

- *Learning is fun*
  Gaining knowledge can be an exciting and stimulating activity in itself. Show your teenager that this is so for you by taking an interest in the subjects he is studying, and asking him to explain things to you. Sharing his newly acquired knowledge with someone who takes a keen interest can be a powerful motivation to acquire more, and the thrill of being able to tell a parent something he/she doesn't know should not be underestimated.

- *I wish I'd done better myself*
  By all means tell your teenager how much you regret not having tried harder at school yourself, and how you feel your life might have been different if you had. Once is probably enough, though – if you make too much of it he may feel that he is simply being asked to fulfil your fantasies, and rebel. Linking his success to something he wants to do will be much more motivating.

- *I'll make it worth your while*
  Although it may go against the grain, the promise of a day out, a gift or even money as a reward for good results can motivate your adolescent where all else has failed. If you consider the parallels with adult life, this bribery really isn't so very shocking. The productivity bonus, the pay rise – indeed, the wage packet – inspire many of us to achieve in our jobs; is this really so very different?

- *To please me*
  Even teenagers are happy to gain their parents' approval, and showing him how pleased and proud you are when he has

tried hard and/or done well will provide a very positive incentive for your adolescent to continue. Putting pressure on him to succeed by threatening to withdraw your affection if he doesn't, will not help, however, and should be avoided.

- *To impress others*
  'What will people think if you fail/drop out?' is not likely to impress your teenager as a reason for doing well at school. He probably feels that the people who matter to him – his friends – don't care much one way or the other, or might even be impressed if he rebelled or dropped out, and he doesn't really care what your friends think anyway.

- *Your sister did better than this*
  Comparing your adolescent's achievements with another's can be especially damaging, particularly within the family. A high-achieving sibling can be a hard act to follow, and the teenager who tries hard within his own abilities but is constantly compared with a more academically able brother or sister may feel that he can never win, so may as well give up. It can be difficult, but try to see each one of your children as individuals and measure them against their own standards.

- *Because I say so*
  This is the fallback position of the exasperated parent, and it really won't wash with most teenagers. If you reach this stage, it is better to end the conversation by saying: 'I think we both need to think seriously about what you can get out of your education. Let's go away and write down everything we can think of for or against your staying on at school (for instance), and then get back together to discuss it again.'

You know your own child, and despite the temptation to make him feel bad about not doing his best, you will probably be able to find some reason that is meaningful to him for making the effort required to achieve his full educational potential.

Gender and motivation

It is generally accepted in the teaching profession that girls are more self-motivated than boys, and this difference becomes increasingly apparent as the gap in development between the sexes widens during puberty. Of course, this is a trend and will not hold true for every child, but there is concern about the number of under-achieving boys, and considerable research and resources have been devoted to trying to rectify this shortfall.

The involvement of either parent has been shown to have a marked effect on their child's educational achievements, but for practical reasons it is more often mothers who take this role. This is fine as far as it goes, but the fact is that boys do not identify themselves with their mothers in quite the way that girls do – they need a male role model who can demonstrate to them the importance of school and the relevance of what they learn there. The best person to achieve this is their father (or another male relative to whom they are close).

There are several ways in which any father can help his son to do better at school, and the first is to have been actively involved in his life throughout his childhood. The degree of involvement a father has with his child (measured by researchers at the ages of seven and eleven) has been shown to influence their number of national exam passes at the age of 16. Children whose fathers have taken an active part in their lives before the age of 11 have also been found to be less likely to have a criminal record by the age of 21 than others. Visiting the school, reading reports, attending parents' evenings, and helping with homework all help to reinforce the positive messages that fathers can give to their sons about the importance of their education.

Even where, perhaps because of pressures of work or because he doesn't live with his son, a father can't get closely involved in his children's education, it is important that he talks to his adolescent about what's happening at school and how he feels about it, and shares his own school experiences with him. Pointing out the practical applications of school subjects, and helping his son to apply them in useful ways in his hobbies, can also help – as can explaining how the skills he learned at school when he was young help in his job, or how they helped him to get the job in the first place.

Of course, all the above points apply just as much to girls as to boys, but the special relationship between father and son means that dads are uniquely placed to help their boys get the most from school. Good schools know and value this, and will enable and welcome constructive input from fathers.

For both boys and girls, there may be academic benefits to be had from a co-educational environment, especially if teachers are aware that they can use gender differences to the benefit of their pupils. Teachers may, for instance, deliberately group boys with girls for certain activities, knowing that the girls will often be more organized in their approach to their work, while the boys may risk a more innovative approach to a problem.

Homework

As children start working towards their GCSE and A-level exams, homework becomes more and more important. How much homework should your teenager be doing? How can you make sure that she is doing it all, and doing it well? How much help should you give?

Government guidelines on homework give a broad indication of how much time secondary school pupils might reasonably be expected to spend on homework per day:

- Years 7 and 8 – 45–90 minutes
- Year 9 – 1–2 hours
- Years 10 and 11 – $1\frac{1}{2}$–$2\frac{1}{2}$ hours

These figures represent a maximum, and the guidelines emphasize that it is more important that the homework is suitable for your child and contributes to his learning than that it fills a certain amount of time. It isn't hard to see, though, that a 15-year-old who is doing $2\frac{1}{2}$ hours of homework per day will have very little time left for his own interests. Adolescents react to this in various ways: some try diligently to do all that is asked of them, to the exclusion of any interests of their own; some do as much as they feel they must to scrape through tests and exams, fitting it around their life outside school; some simply look at what they are expected to achieve and give up.

How can you help your child to find a balance between the requirements of her teachers and her need for a personal and social life during term time?

First, you can find out just how much homework she has been set by looking at her homework diary. Most secondary schools provide their pupils with these diaries – sometimes incorporated in the more general record book. The child uses the diary to record what homework she is given and when it has to be handed in, and many schools require teachers and/or parents to sign the diary on a weekly, or even daily, basis. This shows that everyone is being kept informed about what the child is supposed to be doing, and what she actually does.

There is usually a space for parents to write comments in the homework diary, and you can use this space to let the school know if:

- your child found homework too hard or too easy;
- your child was unable to do the homework for some reason (lost book, etc.);
- homework has not been marked;
- no homework has been set.

If your child is spending a great deal of homework time on a particular subject, it could indicate that she is finding it hard to keep up or to understand the work. Similarly, if she is rushing through her homework in record time, it could indicate that she doesn't fully understand what is required of her. In either case, the first thing to do is to ask the teenager herself for her feelings on the subject. If she is struggling, you or she can let her teacher know by way of the record book, a note or a meeting.

Should you help with homework?

There are several ways in which you can help your child with her homework, short of actually doing it for her. First, and most importantly, you can help simply by being interested. Studies have shown that children do better when their parents take an interest in their work, and simply recognizing your adolescent's efforts and providing encouragement will go a long way towards motivating and rewarding her. Teenagers often seem not to care whether you are interested or not, and affect disdain for good marks or school merit certificates, but your pride in their achievements still matters to them; don't be put off by the rolled eyes and 'Whatever's' – they still need your approval.

You can help in more practical ways too, by providing her with facilities and resources that will help her with her work. You can also do your best to answer any questions she asks you, but beware of the temptation to take over and do her homework for her. It is crucial that she is able to work independently, and this will help her to develop confidence in her own ability to complete the tasks her teachers set her.

DO:
- *Make sure she has somewhere to work*
  She will need a chair and a surface on which to write and spread out her books, in a comfortable room with plenty of light.
- *Ensure she has peace and quiet*
  Although homework is best done away from distractions like the television, most teenagers prefer to have some company, or even a radio playing in the background. Sometimes the kitchen table, with a parent present and available for help if asked, is better than isolation in a bedroom, however good the facilities.
- *Provide basic equipment*
  She will need pens, pencils, crayons, ruler, paper, a calculator and reference material such as an encyclopaedia. If you have a computer and printer, this can be used to produce work and, if you also have a modem, to access the internet for information.
- *Encourage her to do homework at a regular time*
  Early evening, after your child has changed and eaten, but before she is too tired, is a good time for homework.
- *Allow her to work with friends*
  Friends are vitally important to teenagers, and doing home-work together is one way of nurturing friendships while still

getting through the required amount of school work – as children get older it can be hard to find the time for both. New skills are often more easily learned when work is shared, and explaining a difficult concept to someone else can help us to grasp it ourselves.

- *Make sure that finished homework is handed in*
Less organized teenagers may need reminding to hand in their completed homework. A simple verbal checklist before leaving for school will help – 'Have you got your dinner money/PE kit/homework?' The due-date of any given piece of homework should be entered in the homework diary or record book, so a simple check each morning should tell you or your child whether any homework is due in that day.

- *Above all, remember that homework can be fun*
Finding out can be an exciting business, if access to resources such as the local library, museums and the internet is easily available, and sometimes research for homework can spark off new interests and activities for the family. Try to show some enthusiasm when your child asks for your help – whether it is a lift to the library or the use of your computer – and encourage her to find out a bit more than she really needs to know.

DON'T:

- *Take over*
Provide the means to find the information he needs, and help in finding it if necessary, but allow your child to draw his own conclusions and write up the result in his own words – in discussion with you if need be.

- *Pretend you know everything*
Allow your teenager to tell you about what he has learned, admit that he now knows more than you about some subjects, and ask him to explain some of it to you. This will give his confidence an enormous boost.

- *Be too rigid about when homework is done*
Your adolescent needs to take part in other activities outside school and to see his friends sometimes. Very little home-work is due back on the day after it is set, and missing a

homework session from time to time will not matter overly –
he can simply catch up the next day.

- *Assume it is your teenager's fault if he is struggling with his
  homework*
  All homework activities should be related to the work being
  done at school, and schools and teachers are required to
  organize homework carefully so that their pupils are not
  expected to do too much on any one day. If he can't cope, let
  the school know.

Feedback

Few things are more demotivating than to put a great deal of
effort into a piece of work, only to find that it is still unmarked
weeks later, or that the teacher has only skimmed through it, or
given it an almost arbitrary mark. Teachers are often very hard-
pressed, but this is an important issue and they have certain
expectations to live up to. They must give pupils feedback on
their homework, letting them know how well they have done
and how they could do better. This can be done through
discussion in lessons, or through written comments on their
work.

If several pieces of homework in the same subject remain
unmarked, or it appears that a teacher has overlooked serious
mistakes in your child's work, or not given sufficient acknowl-
edgement of his efforts, you should contact the school.

Stress

During the teenage years, just as your child is facing the
pressures and challenges of the transition to adult life, the pace
at school really hots up. At 14 he is called upon to predict his
choice of occupation in adult life and choose the subjects he
will take at GCSE, and then spends the following two years
working towards his exam results. After GCSEs, the pressure
builds up still further – he must either launch himself into the
world of work or spend the next two years working for his A-

levels, and possibly applying for a place at university. All this pressure can result in rising stress levels, and this can have serious consequences for your teenager's mental and physical health. For a description of the signs of stress and for practical measures to tackle it, see Chapter 6.

Most teenagers cope remarkably well with school despite the upheavals of adolescence, and this is at least in part due to the importance of their friendships. What they crave more than anything in this phase of their lives is to spend as much time as possible together, and the saving grace of school is that it enables them to do this, however irksome the environment in which they meet. Things can go badly wrong, however, when friendships break down, or when the child feels isolated or rejected by her peers. In the following chapter, we will explore the issues surrounding bullying – shown in recent studies to be one of the biggest causes of concern for teenagers and parents alike.

5

Bullying

Studies indicate that one in four children will be involved in bullying at school, as bully or victim, and one of the biggest worries for many parents is that their child will be bullied. Studies have also suggested that incidents of bullying are not the occasional, one-off flare-ups that we would like to believe. In fact, the majority of cases of bullying uncovered by several research projects into discipline and behaviour at school lasted for 12 months or more.

Bullying can take many forms, all equally damaging. Name-calling and teasing are the most widespread, with boys moving on to physical bullying, and girls tending to favour social ostracism, writing nasty notes and spreading malicious rumours in their efforts to cause each other hurt and distress.

Although it was once considered a perfectly normal part of growing up, bullying is now acknowledged as a serious problem, and one that affects children's levels of achievement at school and damages their self-esteem, sometimes for life. Unfortunately, adolescents rarely tell their parents that they are being bullied, preferring to share their worries with friends, or coping with them alone. Because it is such a serious problem, parents need to be on the lookout for signs that their child might be caught up in bullying, in or outside school:

- *Withdrawal*
  The bullied child may become quiet and withdrawn, to the point of appearing sullen. He may find it difficult to do anything positive at all, and spend most of his time at home apparently daydreaming or playing computer games, where he can leave behind his doubts about his own ability to cope, and be someone else for a while. Family outings, out-of-school activities and visits to friends may become an ordeal, and he may prefer to stay at home alone.
- *Becoming difficult and argumentative*
  He may have an exaggerated awareness of any unfairness

43

or favouritism within the family, and feel victimized and put upon in circumstances where this is clearly not the case. He may resent any minor criticism or demand on his time out of all proportion to the event – a request to tidy his room, for instance, may provoke protests of 'You're always going on at me – you never tell anyone else to tidy their room!', although this is patently untrue. Underlying these responses is the feeling that 'Everyone's picking on me!'

- *Aggressive behaviour*
  He may 'act out' his anger and frustration by behaving aggressively towards brothers and sisters, or others outside the family. He may pick fights, become overly possessive of belongings, or overreact to the normal, everyday arguments that are an inevitable part of family life. In an attempt to re-establish his damaged self-esteem and confidence, the victim may become a bully himself.
- *Fear of going to school*
  If the bullying is taking place at school, or on the way there, he may refuse to go, ask repeatedly to be driven rather than walking or catching the bus, or develop frequent mystery illnesses. Some victims of bullying will develop full-blown school phobia, where the prospect of going to school is so terrifying that they will beg, plead, threaten and even become physically ill if their parents insist that they go. Persistent truanting can also be a result of bullying.
- *Schoolwork problems*
  Children who are being bullied at school may spend all their time there in a state of fear and apprehension, and not surprisingly their schoolwork may suffer.
- *Missing possessions*
  School books may be damaged or lost and dinner money and possessions may go missing. Sometimes the victim will try to placate the bully by giving him presents or money.
- *Disturbed sleep*
  Nightmares and disturbed sleep may make the bullied teenager reluctant to go to bed and leave him tired in the morning, and it will be quite an effort to get him off to school

on time – particularly as school may be the last place he wants to be.

- *Stealing*

  The adolescent who is the victim of a 'protection racket' may have to steal to satisfy the bully's demands. He may become involved in criminal activity, such as shoplifting, because of threats from others, or because he fears rejection by the group if he doesn't.

- *Injuries*

  Physical bullying may leave obvious bruises which the victim will try to explain away. Injuries incurred in school time and reported to staff, in a PE lesson for instance, will be recorded in the school accident book, so it is possible to check your child's explanations with the school if you suspect that suspiciously frequent injuries have been deliberately inflicted.

- *Low self-esteem*

  The victim of verbal bullying may try desperately to change the attributes that the bullies have picked upon for ridicule, becoming painfully self-conscious about some aspect of her appearance or clothing. Some children deliberately fail in their schoolwork after being called 'teacher's pet', others resort to obsessive washing after being called 'smelly' or 'dirty'.

- *Depression*

  Because their self-image is so fragile and the approval of their peer group so important to them, bullying can be particularly devastating for this age group, and teenagers, like adults, can and do become truly depressed. The depressed or suicidal adolescent needs urgent help – forcing him to school will only make matters worse (see Chapter 6).

Any or all of the above could indicate bullying, but most of them will also be familiar to the parents of teenagers as typical adolescent behaviour, so how will you know if your teenager is being bullied? The signs of adolescence generally appear slowly over weeks or months, so any sudden change in your child's behaviour must be suspect. Any marked change that seems to be associated with a particular event or group could also be significant – if your child seems much happier in holiday time, but becomes anxious as the new term approaches, for instance, problems with bullying may be the explanation.

It is important to give your child every opportunity and encouragement to talk to you about what is worrying her, but this may not be easy. Bullying is an emotive issue, laden for both parent and child with fears of inadequacy, rejection and failure. This can make it a difficult and embarrassing topic of conversation for both, particularly where teenagers are concerned.

Parental concern about bullying, though, is justified and valuable. If you feel that something is wrong, but are finding it difficult to talk to your teenager about it, try approaching the subject in a more general way:

• Tell him about a time when you or a friend were bullied, and what you did about it.
• Ask whether he knows anyone who is being, or has been, bullied, and what the school did about that.
• Ask around the parents of friends – they may have heard something from their own children that will help to shed light on the situation.

Talk to the school

If you think that your teenager is being bullied, or is bullying, at school, it is vitally important that you contact the school as soon as possible. Every school should have an anti-bullying policy that describes how it will deal with incidents of bullying, and should bring this into operation as soon as an incident is reported.

Your first point of contact is your child's form teacher. He or she will have some knowledge of your child, and often of the others involved as well, and is in the best position to assess the situation and suggest remedies. Ask him to:

• investigate your child's complaints;

- keep you informed of the results;
- inform the head teacher of your meeting.

It is important that you approach the meeting or telephone conversation with your child's teacher armed with as much information as possible. Don't rely on your memory – write down all the facts you have gathered so far and all the questions you want to ask, for otherwise you are certain to miss something out. From the first moment you suspect that bullying may be a problem, either you or your child should keep a detailed diary of events, including:

- names of any other pupils involved, including witnesses;
- dates and times of incidents;
- where the incidents took place;
- details of injuries and any treatment received for them;
- details of damage to, or theft of, property.

After each meeting, write to those involved confirming the main points covered and detailing any action agreed upon.

What can I expect the school to do?
- Take the matter seriously.
- Protect your child until the matter can be sorted out.
- Talk to the victim, the bully and witnesses.
- Talk to parents of the bully and of bullied children.
- Take action to prevent further bullying.

My teenager doesn't want to tell

Often parents only find out about bullying in a roundabout way, perhaps from a classmate or parent, or suspect that their child is being bullied but have no concrete proof. Don't be put off, however, if the school says that it is impossible for them to take action without evidence. Names and details make investigation easier, of course, but even if it proves impossible for the school to track down the culprits in this particular incident, there is much that they can do to discourage bullying in more general terms – a warning to the whole school, if made with sufficient conviction and carried through, can be very effective.

If you don't feel that the school is doing enough to prevent bullying, or to protect your child, take your complaint first to the class tutor, then to the head of year, then to the head teacher. If you are still not satisfied, write to the chair of governors. If all these approaches fail, contact the local education authority with your concerns. Do not hesitate to keep your child away from school if you (or he) feel(s) that he is not safe there. Most schools will advise against this, rightly asserting that the longer he stays away, the more difficult it will be for him to return. If they can't assure you, however, that your child will be protected from bullying while he is at school and as he arrives and leaves, or if promises of protection are not fulfilled, there is absolutely no point in forcing a distressed and frightened adolescent back into school for another day of fear and anticipation – he will learn nothing, and the damage caused by the bullying will get steadily more difficult to reverse.

What if the bully is a teacher?

Some teachers still use fear, taunts and humiliation to control their classes; and sometimes a teacher will take a dislike to a particular child, and belittle everything he does, labelling him lazy, badly behaved, or just plain thick. Because children and parents expect teachers to use their authority responsibly, this form of bullying may not be recognized as such, although it is potentially extremely damaging to the child.

If you suspect that your child is being bullied by a particular teacher but isn't telling you, the best approach in the first instance is probably to talk to the teacher concerned. Don't accuse him or her of bullying your child, simply say that you are concerned about how he is getting on and want to ask the teacher's advice. You may be able to gauge his or her attitude by the way he or she responds to your concerns.

If a teacher is bullying your child or others, the situation must be brought to the attention of the school. Often, teachers will be aware of a colleague's methods, but it takes complaints by children and parents to get anything done. A good school will listen to your worries and take action.

Can the police help?

You are quite entitled to ask the police for help, whether or not your child has been physically harmed. The threat or infliction of physical harm, as well as harm to a person's state of mind, constitutes an assault in law. Even if the police decide not to prosecute or caution the bully, some schools liaison officers will make a point of visiting the school and warning pupils of the possible consequences of bullying, which may help to bring its seriousness home to them.

What if your own child is the bully?

Bullying is bad for bullies too. Many begin bullying because of their own low self-esteem, or their anger and distress over problems in their own life, and many do not see their behaviour as bullying at all; in fact, the bully will often see herself as a victim, and the bullying behaviour as a reasonable response. This behaviour needs to be challenged, as there is evidence that it may otherwise continue into adult life and lead to criminal activity. The bully needs help to sort out the problems that have led her to bullying in the first place.

If you are told by the school, or by other parents or children, that your child is bullying, try not react with disbelief and aggression. Talk to your child, as calmly as possible, about the allegations, and try to help her to understand the effect that her behaviour is having on others and its possible consequences for her. These include prosecution by the police, whether actual harm has been done or simply threats made.

See my book *Helping Children Cope with Bullying* (Sheldon Press, 1994) for further information on preventing and dealing with bullying.

6

Health – Mental and Physical

While children are young, it is relatively easy to ensure that they eat the right things, get enough sleep, and aren't exposed to unnecessary health risks. However, things change in adolescence. Probably for the first time in their lives, our children start to make their own decisions and choices, often without reference to us and without our knowledge – from the food they buy, to the places they visit, and the company they keep, an increasingly unknown quantity has been introduced into the equation, and because the adolescent's grasp of the relationship between action and consequence is still developing, their choices may not always be made on the basis of what is best for either their short- or long-term health. Adolescence brings new health problems of its own, too. The following issues commonly cause concern to teenagers, their parents, or both:

- Diet and eating.
- Exercise.
- Stress and depression.
- Menstrual difficulties.
- Skin problems.
- Tobacco, alcohol and drug use (covered in Chapter 11).

Diet and eating

The rapid development that takes place around puberty requires good nutrition as its fuel and building blocks, and a balanced diet is just as important at this age as it was during childhood. There are other reasons for maintaining a healthy diet, too:

- Research has shown that a good diet protects against coronary heart disease and some cancers – diseases that may develop in later life, but can seem distant and irrelevant to the adolescent.
- Once their periods start, girls are at additional risk of developing anaemia. A balanced diet will protect against this.

- A poor diet containing a lot of sugary foods can damage permanent teeth.
- A diet containing too many fatty, starchy foods can contribute to obesity, risking unhappiness and long-term ill health.
- A good diet is essential for energy and activity. Adequate exercise has been shown to improve health and increase the effectiveness of learning.

Unfortunately, emotional issues now come into play. Rejecting the older generation's concept of a desirable diet can become a part of the teenager's struggle for independence and identity. We cannot directly control what our children eat outside the home, and all teenagers will experiment with different diets to some extent, just at they do with different looks and opinions, but we can continue to provide healthy, nutritious food at home, and to set a good example by eating well ourselves.

Here are some practical ways to ensure your teenager gets enough of the foods he needs for good health:

Breakfast

Studies have shown that eating breakfast improves children's problem-solving abilities, memory, concentration levels, visual perception and creative thinking. Teachers, too, are adamant that many children are unable to perform to their full potential at school because they do not eat a proper breakfast.

Unfortunately, breakfast is the one meal that teenagers often miss or rush. Because they find it hard to get up in the morning, they may have neither the time nor the inclination to eat breakfast, and this can leave them with an energy low just when they need to work hardest. To ensure that your child eats a proper breakfast, try these simple measures:

- Wake her early, and repeatedly, in plenty of time for breakfast.
- If she still isn't up in time, give her something portable to eat on the way to school – not ideal, but better than going without.

Whether she eats in comfort or on the run, the ideal breakfast will include complex carbohydrates – wholemeal bread or cereals, for example – which break down more slowly in the body than refined foods, and provide a more consistent release of energy into the bloodstream. Sugared cereals and other very sweet things prompt a quick release of energy, followed by a correspondingly sudden fall in blood sugar later in the morning, which causes tiredness.

Lunch

On school days, there is a choice to be made between packed meals and school dinners. There are points for and against both options:

Packed lunches
IN FAVOUR:

- You know what your teenager is eating.
- Packed meals can work out cheaper than school dinners.
- Special dietary requirements can be catered for (e.g. vegetarian, a dairy allergy).
- She will not need to take money to school – a potential magnet for bullies.

AGAINST:

- Few schools have refrigerated storage for packed lunches, which may stand in a hot classroom for hours before being eaten, with obvious health risks.
- Preparing several packed lunches during the morning rush to get everyone out of the house can be a real burden.
- Thinking of healthy foods that will not deteriorate in the lunch box, and that picky teenagers will actually eat, can be quite a challenge.

School dinners
FOR:

- School dinners can provide a cooked meal at a relatively low price. For some pupils, this is their main meal of the day.
- Sharing a cooked meal with others helps to develop social skills and cement friendships.

- Where the school operates a cafeteria-style system, buying school dinners may help your teenager to learn about budgeting and the value of money.

AGAINST:

- Some adolescents may find that their energy requirements are not met by the standard portion size.
- Although healthy meals may be available, there is often nothing to stop your teenager from choosing chips and a fizzy drink followed by chocolate mousse, for instance, for every meal.
- 'Dinner money' can attract bullies and thieves.

During school holidays and at weekends, what your teenager eats at lunchtime may be dictated by where he is. If he's out with friends, he may well settle for a chocolate bar and a packet of crisps, or miss the meal altogether. As long as he has had a substantial breakfast and will share a family evening meal when he gets home, this isn't likely to cause him any real harm.

The evening meal

Teenagers will often disdain any sort of family gathering, and ask to be allowed to take food up to their room, where they can watch their favourite television 'soap'. If you insist on a sit-down meal, you may be faced with a sullen, silent adolescent whose one aim seems to be to make everyone else's life a misery. The content of the meal itself can also become an issue. This is understandable – children have very little control over their own lives; most major decisions are made for them; the one thing they can decide for themselves is what they do and don't eat. How can we avoid conflict at mealtimes, without making endless work for whoever prepares the food?

- Time the meal when it will not conflict with homework or must-see television programmes.
- Set some basic rules that everyone must observe: no bullying, no bickering and everyone helps to lay and clear the table, for instance. You may also be able to instigate a washing-up rota, though many have tried and failed!

- You can't please all of the people all of the time, so make it clear that anyone who doesn't like what's on offer is welcome to microwave himself a baked potato or boil some pasta – an adequate meal with some cheese and a piece of fruit. The average young teenager is old enough to do this safely after a little instruction.
- Encourage your adolescent to choose and cook a meal for the rest of the family occasionally. Many are flattered to be asked, and the experience can give an insight into the difficulties of cooking for a family. Be nice about it when they do!
- Welcome your teenager's friends to your table. While your own child may consider your meals seriously uncool, his friends will often appreciate home-cooked food – just as long as it isn't cooked in *their* home!

What should your teenager be eating?

A balanced diet must include foods from each of the five main groups, in about the following proportions: fruit and vegetables 30 per cent, bread, cereals and potatoes 30 per cent, meat, fish, pulses, Quorn, etc., 15 per cent, dairy foods 15 per cent, fat and sugary foods 10 per cent. There is lots of choice within these groups, so healthy food need never be boring. Some foods we think of as less healthy, such as chips and burgers, can form a part of a healthy diet, but on their own or eaten frequently they will be far too heavy on fats and refined carbohydrates to provide balanced nutrition.

It wouldn't be realistic to suppose that you could persuade your teenager to forgo fast food and sweets altogether; it is probable that he will go through a phase of experimenting with these before he arrives at a diet that will suit his tastes and needs for life, but his view of what constitutes a normal diet will be most influenced by the food he has grown up with.

Vegetarian eating

It is quite common for teenagers, as part of their new feelings of responsibility for the world around them, to announce that they are becoming vegetarian. While this can be a bit inconvenient in a family whose diet is based on animal proteins, a balanced vegetarian diet is every bit as healthy as a meat-based one.

It is particularly important that changing to a vegetarian diet does not simply mean that your child misses out the meat content of meals without substituting an alternative, and that girls in particular have a suitable source of iron included in their diet, or take an iron supplement, as iron deficiency anaemia is a possible consequence of a poor vegetarian diet.

Eating disorders

At puberty, both boys and girls find that the shape of their bodies is changing dramatically, and there is often a period of distinct chubbiness, often referred to as 'puppy fat', before the teenager's body settles down to its mature, adult shape. Just as all this is happening, the adolescent becomes acutely self-aware, and begins to compare herself with the physical role models presented to her in the media and among her own friends. The natural insecurity of adolescence can lead to great dissatisfaction with this new appearance, and some children, both boys and girls, become so unhappy that they try to stop or change the course of their body's development by starving themselves or eating bizarre types and quantities of food. This goes far beyond issues of faddiness or simple overeating, and can cause real physical and psychological harm. Although girls are more commonly affected, it is important to remember that boys can suffer from eating disorders too.

There are three main classifications of eating disorder:

Anorexia nervosa
The anorexic is terrified of being overweight, and feels fat even when obviously extremely thin. She may have a fascination with food, even though she eats very little herself, and insist on cooking elaborate meals for the rest of the family. Often the anorexic will eat only a very limited range of foods – perhaps salads or fruit – and seems unable to understand that this is not sufficient to keep her healthy. She may exercise, take laxatives

or make herself sick in order to lose more weight, and girls may stop menstruating as their body weight falls.

Bulimia nervosa

Bulimics eat very large amounts of food and then make themselves sick, and although their weight may remain normal, they can eventually suffer serious physical harm as a result of their continuous cycle of eating and vomiting. They may also diet sporadically and take laxatives in order to lose weight.

Compulsive eating

Compulsive eaters use food for comfort or as a distraction from their problems, and habitually eat far more than they need. This long-term overeating results in serious obesity, which can be damaging to health and self-esteem.

If you suspect that your child is developing an eating disorder, it is important that you seek help from your family doctor. See Useful Addresses at the back of this book for sources of further help.

Exercise

The amount of exercise that children take spontaneously declines as they mature, and it is particularly important that adolescents are encouraged to take part in physical activities. Girls tend to decrease the amount of exercise they take in adolescence even more than boys, who remain more active throughout.

How much exercise does your teenager need to maintain good health?

The Health Education Authority (HEA) makes the following recommendations:

- All young people should participate in one hour per day of moderate physical activity.
- Young people who currently do little activity should participate in physical activity of at least moderate intensity for at least half an hour per day.

- Done at least twice a week, some of these activities should help to enhance and maintain muscular strength and flexibility and bone health.

This should be enough, according to the HEA, to:

- Optimize physical fitness, current health, and growth and development.
- Reduce the risk of chronic diseases later in life.
- Develop active lifestyles at an early age to encourage a lifelong exercise habit.

Teenagers do not need to take part in very strenuous activity to gain health benefits; moderate levels of activity equivalent to brisk walking are quite sufficient to count towards the target. Walking to and from school, where it is possible and safe to do so, can therefore fulfil part or all of this daily exercise requirement.

The National Curriculum requires schools to promote physical activity and healthy lifestyles through PE lessons. By the time they have been at secondary school for a couple of years, however, most teenagers have gravitated towards one of two groups – the sporty and the non-sporty types. Those who are interested in sport will probably be taking part in it both outside school and as an extra school activity, and those who are not may be so unenthusiastic and resistant about PE that it probably does them very little good. Because of this, it would not be realistic to expect school to make more than a small contribution to your child's overall exercise requirement, and anything that you can do to encourage him to take part in physical activities outside school can only benefit his health. Try:

- encouraging him to walk or cycle to and from school;
- encouraging him to try new activities with a physical element – paintballing, skateboarding and golf, for instance, all involve exercise, and may attract the adolescent who wouldn't be seen dead taking part in team games or athletics;
- taking exercise as a family at weekends (walking, cycling, swimming, etc.);

- resisting pressure to drive him everywhere he wants to go, where it is safe for him to get there under his own steam.

Stress and depression

Stress

Stress is a natural reaction to challenging circumstances, and the physical changes it induces – increased adrenaline production and heart rate, a rush of energy and so on – prepare us for 'fight or flight'. In certain circumstances, for instance the start of a sporting competition or a difficult interview, this can help us to give of our best. When stress is prolonged, however, it can lead to physical and emotional problems.

Adolescence is a stressful time for the maturing individual, and it is important that parents can recognize the symptoms of stress, and act to relieve it when it occurs. Adolescents who are subject to prolonged periods of stress can, just like adults, lapse into depression or ill health and lose the confidence and motivation to take on the challenges of life. The following signs can be indicators that your teenager is under more stress than she can easily cope with:

- Physical tension – being 'like a coiled spring'.
- Difficulty in sleeping.
- Increased susceptibility to minor infections – colds, sore throats, skin rashes, etc.
- Irritability.

It may be obvious what is causing her stress reaction – exams, family arguments, etc. – but if it is not, try to talk to your child about what is worrying her. Make an appointment to talk to her class tutor, too – he may be able to tell you of a problem at school that your child hasn't mentioned to you. Even if she doesn't want to talk about her current problem, you can help by talking generally about stress and how to handle it, and reassuring her that she is doing OK as far as you are concerned, and needn't face any problems alone.

As we get older, we all learn to cope with stress, to a greater or lesser extent. For the teenager facing stressful events for the first time, however, the temptation may be to avoid or escape from the stressful situation, perhaps even turning to drugs or alcohol in an attempt to cope, or to pretend that it is not happening. This doesn't work as a long-term strategy, however, as it is impossible to master any new skills or face challenges without experiencing some degree of stress. The key is to learn to face stress positively. Here are some suggestions that you can make to your stressed child:

- Remember that everyone gets stressed at times – there is nothing wrong with you.
- Confronting your stressful situation and doing your best will make you feel much better about yourself, even if you are not successful, than running away – and the situation will be far less difficult the next time.
- Learning self-relaxation techniques can help you to cope with stressful moments.
- Listing the reasons why you are well equipped to face this challenge can help you to view it more positively: 'I always get good marks in this subject', 'I have trained hard for this competition', 'I am good at sticking up for myself without losing my temper'.
- Even if things go badly, you still have a family that loves and admires you, and respects you for having a go.

Bullying, parents' relationship problems, or marital breakdown, loneliness and feelings of inadequacy, and many other common situations, can cause teenagers stress from which they cannot find relief without help. In these cases, parents must take a hand to tackle the cause of the stress directly, or find the help that the child needs from outside sources. Your doctor's surgery or library should be able to tell you about local sources of help and counselling for young people.

Depression

True depression is more than just feeling a bit low or unhappy – it is a serious condition that can prevent the sufferer from getting on with his life, and leave him feeling that there is no hope for the future, and no point in carrying on. Teenagers can and do become depressed, and it is important that parents are able to recognize the signs, which can include some (but not usually all) of the following:

- A general feeling of misery.
- Moodiness – often with a clear pattern in which the sufferer always feels worse in the morning and better as the day goes on, or vice versa.
- Disturbed sleep, or sleeping much more than usual.
- Anxiety.
- Irritability.
- Lack of energy.
- Thinking, speaking and moving more slowly than usual.
- Difficulty concentrating, or deterioration of schoolwork.
- Forgetfulness.
- Inability to enjoy things that are normally fun.
- Worries about the future – feelings of hopelessness.
- Low self-esteem and guilt.
- Failure to look after oneself properly – washing or brushing hair, etc.
- Hypochondria.
- Loss of appetite or overeating.
- Severely depressed teenagers may try to harm themselves or take their own life.

The signs of depression could easily be mistaken for the normal ups and downs of adolescence, and vice versa, but there are differences. If symptoms persist over a long period to the point where they interfere with the teenager's day-to-day life and his relationships with others, if his 'downs' are no longer balanced by 'ups', the possibility that he is suffering from a depressive illness needs investigation.

Why do teenagers get depressed?

Sometimes a traumatic incident, either in their personal lives – like an argument with a friend or, on a wider scale, like the terrorist attacks on New York's World Trade Center – can overwhelm the teenager's ability to cope, triggering off a depressive illness. Sometimes, though, there is no obvious reason; things simply get on top of her and she feels she can't handle them. Adolescents' resources may already be stretched almost to breaking point. They lack the ability to shut out the painful feelings and experiences that we all face from time to time, and cannot help dwelling on the great injustices and sadnesses of life.

There is a correlation between depression and substance abuse in young people, though not a clear causal relationship. Girls are twice as likely as boys to become depressed, although boys are more likely to attempt suicide than girls (see below). A family history of depressive illness seems to make depression in children and young people more likely. Long-term stress can also lead to depression, and children struggling with learning difficulties can become depressed, as can those suffering from a chronic illness or disability.

Who can help?

Depression is not caught like a cold, and there is usually a progression over time from simply feeling a bit low to a full-blown depressive illness. There is a great deal that family and friends can do in the early stages to help the sufferer to avoid long-term depression, simply by encouraging him to talk about his worries and listening sympathetically and supportively. Sometimes, though, it is difficult for the teenager concerned to talk to someone in the family, or even to one of his friends (although this is usually easier). There is help available from the Youth Counselling Service and Child Guidance Clinics, and telephone counselling services like ChildLine can also offer support (see Useful Addresses at the back of this book). If you think that your child is sliding towards depression, it is important to tackle the problem before it becomes more serious. Talk to your GP, who will be able to suggest sources of counselling or other help.

Teenage suicides

In the United Kingdom, there are about 13 suicide deaths each year in the 15–19 age group, although hospital attendances resulting from suicide attempts run into the thousands. Young men are more likely to attempt suicide than young women, perhaps because they are less likely to show signs of distress or to talk about their feelings before they reach this point.

Suicide attempts may be linked to existing depression or other mental illness, but in about one in five cases there had been no previous sign of emotional or behavioural problems. Sometimes a teenager is just overwhelmed by events – perhaps exam stress, rejection by a girlfriend, and an argument with his parents all come at once, and he simply doesn't have the life experience or resources to cope. Using drugs or alcohol to escape from his problems may simply make matters worse, and can make a suicide attempt more likely.

Sometimes, the adolescent attempting suicide simply wants to show everyone how bad or angry he is feeling. Lacking the communication skills and self-knowledge to recognize and explain his problems, he may feel that this is the only way for him to make his point and be taken seriously. However, this doesn't mean that he should be seen simply as an 'attention seeker' – he still needs help to deal with his problems, and there is a real risk that he will attempt suicide again – perhaps successfully this time – if he doesn't get the support he needs.

How can parents help?

- Notice when your teenager seems upset and encourage him to talk about what's wrong. Just knowing that you care, even if he doesn't want to talk about what's on his mind, will help.
- If he doesn't want to talk to you, suggest other sources of help (see Useful Addresses at the back of this book) and make it possible for him to access them.
- If he talks of suicide or not wanting to live, take him very seriously.
- A substantial proportion of teenage suicides involve over-the-counter drugs like paracetamol, which affects the liver and can be lethal even in low doses. Buy them in small quantities in blister packs, which discourage impulsive suicide attempts, and keep them locked away where possible.
- If he tells you, or you suspect, that he has taken an overdose, get him to hospital without delay, as even a small dose of

some drugs can do damage that may not be immediately apparent.

- Any teenager who has made a suicide attempt should be assessed by a mental health specialist before he is discharged from hospital. With treatment, most young people will not attempt suicide again, but a few may need specialist, long-term help for depression or other mental health problems.

Menstrual difficulties

Early periods are often irregular and period pain is common. The menstrual cycle should settle down eventually to a more predictable pattern, although it may take a year or more to do so, and pain associated with periods may also diminish or disappear altogether. If pain is severe and persistent, however, a doctor or complementary health practitioner may be able to help. Simple, self-help measures to help with period pain include:

- Gentle exercise, such as walking – some women find that this reduces cramping pain.
- Rest lying on the back, with a hot water bottle on the painful area and a pillow supporting the knees.
- Gentle massage of the painful area.
- Drinking plenty of fluids.
- Lying in a warm bath.
- Painkillers – over-the-counter preparations like ibuprofen may be sufficient, but stronger painkillers are available on prescription for severe pain.

The worry that a period may start unexpectedly, resulting in embarrassment, can be a serious concern for some girls, and they may need reassurance that their menstrual and pre-menstrual symptoms are normal. Keeping a record of their periods can help them to predict bad days and feel more in control. The emotional ups and downs of the menstrual cycle, too, can be confusing and worrying, and can become less of a concern when the correlation with her periods is clear.

Anaemia

Iron deficiency anaemia is thought to be the most common nutritional deficiency in the world, and it is estimated that in the United Kingdom about 4 per cent of adolescent boys and 11 per cent of adolescent girls are anaemic. Women, though, are more commonly affected than men because of their menstrual blood loss. The rapid growth that takes place during puberty raises the iron requirement, making anaemia more likely.

The symptoms of anaemia include:

- Tiredness.
- Irritability.
- Pallor.
- Difficulty in concentrating.
- Lack of stamina.
- Breathlessness.
- Headaches.
- Insomnia.
- Lowered resistance to infection.

Studies have shown that anaemia can impair the ability to learn effectively, and can affect behaviour and development in children, so it is important that parents and adolescents are aware of the risk of becoming anaemic, and know how to avoid it.

A good, balanced diet should provide all the iron that most people need, although girls with very heavy periods may have a higher iron requirement than the average and need to take iron supplements. Iron from animal sources is more easily absorbed than that from plant sources, but it is quite possible to get sufficient iron for normal requirements from a good vegetarian diet. All the following foods are good sources of iron:

- Red meat and offal.
- Eggs.
- Wholegrain cereals.
- Leafy green vegetables.

- Molasses.
- Nuts.
- Pulses (beans, lentils, etc.).
- Some dried fruits.

Vitamin C increases the absorption of iron from food, so it is a good idea to include a source of vitamin C, such as citrus fruits, green peppers or fresh leafy green vegetables, with meals containing a source of iron. Tea can reduce the amount of iron absorbed, so it is best to avoid drinking it with a meal. All white flour in the United Kingdom must, by law, be fortified with iron, and many breakfast cereals also have iron added to them. Because of this, a breakfast of iron-fortified cereal, toast and orange juice is a good way of topping up iron reserves for the day.

Skin problems

Everyone gets spots from time to time, but during adolescence an increase in the secretion in the skin of an oily substance called sebum can cause pores to become blocked. Sebum turns black when exposed to air, causing blackheads, and whiteheads are simply accumulations of sebum trapped under the surface of the skin. When blackheads or whiteheads become infected, the result is an inflamed-looking, swollen spot, and acne is simply a serious case of infected spots.

Stress can cause spots and acne to flare up, hence the frequent appearance of a particularly nasty spot before a date or job interview. There are some simple measures that can help to reduce the appearance of spots:

- Wash the face often with a mild soap and warm water.
- Wash the hair often, reducing the amount of oil transferred to the face and neck.
- Use steam or a face pack to open the pores and reduce sebum.
- Save make-up for special occasions; it can block pores and lead to more spots.

- Avoid excessively greasy foods.
- Eat plenty of fresh fruit and vegetables.
- Drink lots of water.
- Expose the skin to fresh air and sunlight (sun protection creams should still be used, but avoid the greasiest, waterproof ones, reapplying a lighter one frequently instead).
- Use a proprietary spot cream or wash, although it is advisable to try them on a small area of skin first, as they can be rather harsh and cause a reaction.

Serious outbreaks of acne, which may appear on the upper body and neck as well as the face, can make a teenager's life miserable and may cause scarring – particularly if the sufferer picks at or squeezes the spots. If your teenager has a serious problem with spots, he can get help from the family GP, who may give him a course of antibiotics to help clear them up, or from a complementary health practitioner such as a homeopath.

The family doctor

Most teenagers will be registered with the same GP as the rest of the family, often a doctor whom they have got to know over many years. This doesn't mean that the doctor will necessarily report to parents on matters concerning their teenager. Anyone under the age of 16 is entitled to ask for a confidential consultation with his doctor, although the doctor may refuse to treat him on this basis if she thinks that his parents should be informed. After 16, the doctor has the same duty of confidentiality to her teenage patient as to any other.

What if your adolescent doesn't like your family doctor, or finds her difficult to talk to about some things? In most practices, patients are not obliged to see the doctor they are registered with, and can ask for an appointment with another at the same surgery. Anyone over 16 can choose and register with their own GP, and need not get consent from their parents to do so. Under 16, children must be registered by a parent.

Under-16s can give their own consent to medical treatment,

provided they fully understand its implications. If the doctor concerned decides that they do not, a parent, or someone with parental responsibility, can give consent for the proposed treatment.

Parents may feel that they should be involved in their adolescent's medical treatment, if only to ensure that they understand the advice they are given, but we have to remember that teenagers' bodies are entirely their own. We want them to take responsibility for looking after their bodies – by avoiding harmful activities like smoking and drinking, keeping out of potentially dangerous situations, taking precautions to avoid pregnancy and sexually transmitted diseases – but our reluctance to let them go to the doctor alone implies that we don't trust them to make sensible, informed decisions that affect their physical welfare. The teenager might reasonably protest that we can't have it both ways. Perhaps the best course of action, from the age when your child starts to seek some privacy within the family and becomes self-conscious about his body, is to ask him whether he would like you to see the doctor with him, and respect his wishes if he says no. He is more likely to discuss his treatment with you voluntarily if he feels that you trust him to do the right thing.

7

The Wider World

Children need the safety and security of a loving family, and in the early years this is where a child's sense of identity and belonging is centred. As she enters puberty, however, this begins to change. She needs, now, to distance herself from her family, making the space to find her own identity, and friends from among her peer group begin to form the focus of her life.

By around the age of ten, children have started to split themselves into groups of like-minded, same-sex individuals, and to establish very clearly defined rules of dress and conduct – shared tastes in music, television, film and books, sometimes even language – that members must adhere to if they want to continue to be accepted by the group. Shared secrets and confidences help to hold these groups together, and children no longer tell their parents everything that they think and feel, preferring to talk about some aspects of their lives to those who share their experiences – their peers. Though friends will always be important, it is reassuring to know that, as long as the difficult teenage years are handled sensitively and a really serious breach is avoided, most teenagers grow closer to their parents again once they are secure in their own identity and place in the world.

Teenagers and friends

It can be hard to see your child closing off parts of her life and her thoughts to you, but it is essential that parents understand and acknowledge the all-important role that friends play in the life of their adolescent. This role is rather different depending on the gender of the child:

Boys' friendships
Boys' friendships tend to centre more on doing than on feeling. They will often share a common interest, perhaps a sport or a style of music, and their meetings will focus on either taking

part in or talking about this – and, increasingly as puberty progresses, talking about girls. Boys will not often talk to one another about problems or worries that might be interpreted by the group as a sign of weakness, although really close friends can be concerned for one another in a crisis.

As groups of boys tend to focus on activity, there is always the danger that, if they haven't got anything constructive to do, they will find ways of occupying themselves that are less desirable – dangerous acts of bravado, vandalism, and even petty crime being obvious examples. Because they fear losing face with their peers, boys will sometimes do things in groups that they wouldn't dream of doing alone.

Girls' friendships

Girls' friendships focus on sharing feelings and asking opinions rather than a particular activity. Experimenting with hairstyles, make-up and clothes, talking about relationships, sharing problems and, of course, talking about boys, become the focus of their gatherings.

Because 'doing' is not so important to girls, they are less likely than boys to become involved in undesirable or dangerous activities, but it is by no means unheard of for this to happen.

Where should teenagers socialize?

With limited spending power and few public places that welcome gangs of teenagers, most groups of friends are forced to spend time either in one another's houses or on the proverbial 'street corners' – places like parks and shopping malls where access is free and behaviour largely unsupervised. The very lack of adult supervision that draws them to these places can, however, mean that undesirable behaviour goes unchecked, and the youngsters themselves may fall prey to bullies, drug dealers or other individuals who do not have their best interests at heart. This doesn't mean that your teenager should never be allowed out on his own, but it is important to talk to him first about what constitutes acceptable behaviour, what the consequences of unacceptable behaviour may be, and about the risks that strangers can pose – and reminding him of these things often, although he will almost certainly protest when you do.

Inconvenient though it may be for the rest of the family, there are advantages in having your teenager and his friends 'hanging out' in your own home:

- You will know where he is and what he's doing.
- The behaviour of the group will be supervised.
- You will get to know his friends.

Friends are so important to our child that we really need to know something of them and his relationship with them in order to understand what is going on in his life. It's not always easy to get to know teenagers, however, and we may have to be prepared to adopt a role as the tireless provider of snacks and lifts in order to gather some insights into our teenagers' social contacts. Mothers often seem to find this easier than fathers, whose territorial instincts may make it hard for them to accept an invasion of loud, sometimes surly, youths into their property.

Even if your home is a welcoming, friendly place, your teenager and his friends will soon want to spread their wings and get out into the wider world. Some children, particularly those who have grown up in an urban area, will already be travelling confidently on public transport, getting themselves to and from school and the shops alone, long before their thirteenth birthday – for others, the whole process can look quite daunting, although they may be reluctant to admit this and choose to stay at home rather than tackle the challenge of going out alone. You can help your child to build the confidence and skills he needs:

- Travel with him on public transport before he attempts it alone, so that he understands the timetables and procedures.
- Make sure he knows the geography of your area and any he is likely to visit, and can find the bus stops or railway station easily.

- Take him shopping with you, but shop independently, arranging to meet and travel home together.
- Run through the procedure for getting help if anything goes wrong while he's out alone.

Most teenagers will be more confident, and are probably safer, if they take a friend along on their first few independent trips.

Once children start to go out without adult supervision, it is important to establish some ground rules – not only for the reassurance and convenience of their parents, but because the child himself needs the security of a framework within which to choose his activities. Total freedom, with all its attendant risk and responsibility, is a burden that the adolescent is not ready or equipped to carry. Some rules are obvious and universal: before leaving, your child should always tell you where she is going and what time she will be back, and must inform you of any changes of plan or delays as soon as possible. Others, such as the time by which they must always be home, will vary from family to family, and with the age and experience of the adolescent, and be renegotiated and eventually phased out as she matures.

All children who are old enough to be out of your sight for any length of time should have been taught about 'stranger danger', and teenagers should also know at least the basic avoidance techniques of self-defence. There are a number of good self-defence books on the market, any of which would make a good present for a teenager setting out on her first independent outings (see Further Reading at the back of this book).

Setting boundaries

Perhaps the most difficult part of parenting a teenager is setting boundaries. We know (and so do they) that there have to be some rules, but where to set them? If we seek to avoid conflict, we end up giving way over things that we know we should make a stand on. If we play the Victorian parent, we not only deny our child the opportunity to learn gradually to take responsibility for his own affairs, we run the risk of alienating him altogether, inviting total rebellion and making it impossible for him to turn to us when he really needs help.

Teenagers are aware of the difference between issues of authority and the more crucial issues of safety. As long as it is obviously based on love and concern, they do usually acknowledge their parents' continuing responsibility, and value their interest in their welfare. This doesn't mean they won't try to push family boundaries, however, and they need you to be reasonable but firm in response. There has to be some give and take in matters where it is appropriate, and a willingness to renegotiate rules as they grow in age, experience and confidence, but the parent who caves in over every issue leaves the teenager anchorless, with no point of reference, in an uncharted ocean of new experiences and emotions. The result may well be the teenager's increasingly extreme behaviour, as she struggles to elicit some sort of solid, unchanging response that she can get a toehold on.

To provide teenagers with the security they still need and parents with some peace of mind, then, families need some basic rules of behaviour to cover the really important aspects of family life – things that affect the physical, emotional and economic safety, health and well-being of the family, and others outside the family. They don't have to be written down, but they must be discussed and understood by everyone. These may include issues of:

- Privacy – e.g. knocking on bedroom doors, not reading others' letters or diaries.
- Responsible behaviour – e.g. everyone must be in by an agreed time, late nights only on evenings when there is no school the next day, etc.
- Physical restraint – e.g. no hitting or throwing things, however intense the argument.
- Fiscal restraint – e.g. no one runs up the telephone bill without asking first.

They would not include matters of personal choice, e.g.:

- Choice of clothing.
- Choice of music (though they may cover how loudly it is played).
- Disposal of personal funds (pocket money and weekend earnings).

It is important that what rules you do have are simple and clear, and allow for the intervention of unforeseen circumstances.

Sanctions

So, you've established a few, carefully chosen and mutually agreed family rules. What happens when your teenager breaks them? It's not a question of missing a treat or stopping pocket money any more – although those sanctions may still work as deterrents to some extent for younger teenagers, provided this is discussed before the event. Instead, we now rely on our children to keep the rules because they see the sense in them, agreed to them, and don't want to let you or themselves down. If your relationship with your child is generally good and the family's ground rules reasonable, your teenager will probably regret his lapses and fear your displeasure. It may only be necessary for you to reiterate the reasons for the existence of the rules, and make it quite clear that you expected, and expect, better of him. Showing that you expect and believe that your adolescent will do the right thing is vitally important – like the rest of us, his instinct will be to live up (or down) to expectations. His faith in himself is based upon your faith in him.

Friends and peer pressure

Surveys of teenagers and their parents have shown that peer pressure is probably not as significant a factor in the behaviour of adolescents as parents may fear. Teenagers generally gravitate towards others with similar backgrounds, interests and outlook on life, so the troubled teenager may be drawn to other unhappy or disaffected individuals. Since young people with these problems are known to be more prone to involvement in dangerous or antisocial behaviour, a group like this is more likely than average to get into trouble. The problem, though, is not created by the peer group – it is simply an element in what drew the group together in the first place.

Confidence, self-esteem and a sense of responsibility are the teenager's best defence against pressure to join others in risky or unacceptable behaviour, and these qualities are nourished by parents who love, like and trust their child, and encourage her to make thoughtful decisions by providing her with information and the opportunity to talk about important issues.

Relating to the opposite sex

With the onset of puberty, the child's attitude to the opposite sex starts to change. At first, early in puberty at around the age of ten or so, boys and girls split decisively into separate camps. Friendships across the gender divide are rare, and each sex gives every appearance of loathing the other for a good deal of the time. Their differences are emphasized by their uneven development, with girls drawing ahead of boys of their own age physically, emotionally and in educational terms, so that classmates may seem to have little in common and friendships are rare.

As puberty progresses, however, things change. Both girls and boys begin to develop a keen interest in the opposite sex. At first, this interest is largely distant and theoretical, and 'going out' means a few exchanged glances in the playground or, at most, a little surreptitious hand-holding. While there are certainly a few sexually precocious 12- and 13-year-olds, for the majority, the full-blown, adult sexual relationship is a long time – and many tentative, exploratory steps and setbacks – away. Most are not ready, and know it.

Sooner or later, however, it is likely that parents will be faced with their son's or daughter's first girlfriend or boyfriend. The experience can be surprisingly difficult – we may feel, before the event, that we will be able to accept our child's choice with equanimity, but the reality may strain our tolerance more than we expected. For a start, their friends are likely to be teenagers too, struggling with the same insecurities and angst as our own teenager. They may find it hard to interact with us, unsure how they should behave with the parents of a boyfriend/girlfriend, and we may not be much help if this is our own first experience of the relationship. It is important not to overreact. Your teenager may find your criticism of her choice of friend offensive and intolerable, as Ian found when he complained to his daughter Katie, 15, that he found her boyfriend rude and uncommunicative:

> Katie, normally an even-tempered girl who had shown no hint of teenage angst, screamed and swore at me, then swept from the room. Later she quietly repeated some of the things she'd screamed. This time, I heard her. What it boiled down to was, 'When you insult my friends, you insult me by implying that I am too stupid to choose them myself. Don't judge them too hastily, and don't forget that they're young too – I'm probably the same with his family.' I looked at him, and her subsequent boyfriends, in a new way after that, and I could see that their awkwardness was largely due to their youth and embarrassment. Most of all, though, I have learned to trust Katie's judgement – she's not going to end up marrying someone awful just because I failed to point out his faults to her.

Of course, not all the friends of the opposite sex that our teenager talks about or brings home will fall into the category of boyfriend or girlfriend. It isn't always easy for teenagers to make friends of the opposite sex, but when they do, such friendships are often deep and supportive, and help to broaden the teenager's understanding of and respect for the opposite sex. Because, in these friendships and in their relationships with boyfriends/girlfriends, they are still relatively tentative and unsure of themselves, even minor teasing and derogatory comments can be extremely upsetting and hurtful for teenagers, especially when it comes from parents.

The disabled teenager

Finding their place in the world outside the family is a challenge for all teenagers, but for the teenager with a disability there are additional problems. The education system segregates a high proportion of disabled children into special schools, often far from their homes, effectively preventing them from integrating with their able-bodied neighbours, and difficulties of access often make it hard or impossible for them to go to the places where teenage social life is centred. The disability charity Scope highlights the following consequences of social exclusion resulting from their disability as being particularly hard for teenagers to deal with:

- Not being listened to.
- Having no friends.
- Finding it difficult to do the kinds of things that other young people of their age do – such as shopping, going to the cinema, clubbing, etc.
- Being made to feel they have no contribution to make, or that they are a burden.
- Feeling unsafe; being harassed and bullied.
- Not having control over spending money; not having enough money.

The integration of children with special needs into mainstream schools is gradually increasing, and recognition of the need and right of disabled people to have equal access to jobs, services and public places is on the agenda, but change is slow. We can all help by talking to our children about disability, and the effects that social exclusion has on disabled people of their own age and others. For sources of information and support for disabled teenagers and their parents, see Useful Addresses at the back of this book.

Teenagers and the internet

The internet is an unparalleled research tool, giving access to an enormous amount of useful and stimulating material and offering the opportunity to communicate with people all over the world, but this resource for communication and research comes at a price:

- Alongside its useful content, the World Wide Web contains pornographic, violent and otherwise unpleasant, upsetting or downright repellent material.
- Because their judgement of people and situations is immature, teenagers may meet paedophiles or other dangerous individuals through their use of chat rooms, and be manipulated into meeting them or giving them personal information. These potential abusers will often pose as teenagers themselves.
- It is possible to waste considerable amounts of time and money on the internet, browsing through the vast amount of pointless and trivial material that exists alongside the worthwhile content.

There are several ways in which you can monitor and control your teenager's use of the internet:

Keep an eye on things

Site the computer somewhere you can see it – a family room rather than a child's bedroom, for example. You can then check occasionally on the sites your children are accessing, and they will be less tempted to look for material that you would rather they didn't see.

Set up family rules

Once you have explained to your children the dangers of using the internet, you can as a family agree rules covering its use. These could include such things as the times at which the internet can be accessed, what it can be used for and who can use it, as well as a family policy concerning the use by older children of sites with violent or sexual content when younger children are around. No one should ever give their full name, address or telephone number to anyone they meet in a chat room or newsgroup.

Use software that filters out adult content

Many internet service providers (ISPs) offer free software that aims to filter out sites containing material unsuitable for children, or it can be purchased independently of your ISP. This software is not infallible, however, and some supervision is still essential.

'Spam'

'Spam' is advertising or marketing material sent out via e-mail. Because this form of advertising costs very little, such material is often sent out randomly and to vast numbers of e-mail addresses. Most spam is simply a nuisance, cluttering up mailboxes and taking time to read and delete, but some contains hard-core pornographic images. It is possible to set up rules in your e-mail software that will filter out messages containing certain words, usually sending them to a separate folder for deletion, but this does sometimes eliminate quite innocent messages that just happen to contain one of the words you have specified, and may miss some that contain offensive graphics but not the trigger words. If your teenager has a separate e-mail address, you might want to consider setting up such rules for his address.

Some spam contains programs that run automatically when the message is opened, and which take the user straight to a site containing pornographic images. It is possible, in most browsers or by using anti-virus or internet security software, to prevent such programs from running automatically, although such precautionary measures can also prevent the user from accessing some perfectly innocent websites. All in all, there is, at the time of writing, no completely reliable or trouble-free defence against pornographic spam, and the most reliable way of avoiding it is to take every possible precaution to keep your e-mail address private, and to change addresses once 'spammers' have found your existing one. This problem is taken very seriously by internet service providers and governments, however, and new measures to tackle it are constantly being sought. See Useful Addresses at the back of this book for sources of further information.

If your teenager accidentally comes across text or images that are unpleasant or disturbing, it is important that she can talk to you about what she has seen without being blamed for seeing it. Reassure her that it is not her fault, and try to deal with any worries she may have as a result of what she has seen; for example, she may need to know that scenes of rape or other violence are almost certainly not genuine, but performed by consenting adults who were paid for their services.

8

Becoming Independent

We don't become independent overnight when we reach the age of legal majority; from the moment we leave the womb, we are moving away from complete dependence on our mother, father and whoever else fills the role of parents in our lives. In a series of small steps, we test and loosen the bonds that tie us to them, until eventually we can achieve independence. We do this with varying degrees of success, and none of us ever escapes completely the effects of those early years with our parents; they remain, at the core of our personality, for the rest of our lives.

One of the most important and difficult skills of parenting is finding a balance between the urge to protect one's child and the child's need for independence. When they are very young it is relatively easy – the benefits to your toddler of poking a pencil in the electric socket or climbing inside the washing machine clearly do not outweigh the risks; allowing a six-year-old to cross a busy road alone would clearly be irresponsible. As children enter puberty, however, the dividing line between acceptable risk and overprotection becomes less clear. Should your 11-year-old travel to a friend's house on the other side of town alone? Will your 14-year-old be able to handle a date with a 19-year-old? It's no longer a matter of sending them to the corner shop to spend their pocket money while you watch from the front doorstep; your child will be loose in the wide, adult world, and you just won't be there to sort things out if they go wrong.

Although there are some activities that are curtailed in law before a certain age, it is simply not possible to lay down any hard and fast rules about the age at which adolescents are ready to pass any one of countless milestones of independence. Some things are never completely safe, and as adults we take risks every day, often without a second thought. Though our instinct is to protect our children from *all* possible harm, we have to accept that this is just not possible, and concentrate on giving them the information, experience and, above all, the conviction of self-worth to avoid unnecessary risk and to handle difficult or dangerous situations in an adult way when they do arise. This process starts early – even before adolescence – and involves a continual re-evaluation of our children's growing maturity and an open-minded approach to changes in the way the family has 'always done' things.

If we are to make sensible decisions about the amount of independence to allow our teenagers, it will help to look in advance at the sort of activities they might propose taking part in and how we can reasonably assess the risk they present. Among the areas that commonly cause conflict between parents and younger teenagers are the following:

Curfews

Once your adolescent has established that he can go out without you, the question of curfews will not be far behind. By what time should teenagers be home? Several factors will influence your decision:

- Will she have to be up and fully functioning early the following morning for school?
- Will she have to walk or cycle home in the dark, or through isolated areas, after a certain hour?
- If you are collecting her by car, will younger children have to be kept up, and taken along?
- Even if you aren't collecting, you will not be able to sleep until she gets home. How late can you comfortably stay up?

Obviously things change a good deal between the ages of 11, when puberty may already have kicked in, and 18, when your adolescent legally becomes an adult, but it is reasonable at any age to expect the young person concerned to be considerate of his family's concerns and convenience.

Parties

We've all heard horror stories about gatecrashers, spiked drinks, drug dealers and fights, and we know that the most innocent of teenage parties can go spectacularly wrong if it's infiltrated by a couple of kids hell-bent on making mischief. In reality, though, most early teenage parties are rather tame affairs – boys and girls are often still so uncomfortable with one another and so fraught with self-consciousness and anxiety that they spend the whole evening sitting in the corner with their best friend. When your 13-year-old tells you that she's been asked to a party, though, here are a few questions to ask before you make up your mind:

- Is the invitation from someone your child knows well, and whose parents you know, or a casual invitation from an acquaintance?
- Will others at the party be of a similar age to your child, older or younger?
- Will it be held at a private house or a public venue such as a village hall or community centre?
- Will there be adult supervision?
- Will alcohol be available?

You can come to a decision based upon the answers to these questions and your knowledge of their friends, weighed against the age and experience of your child, but there is one very important proviso: whatever his age, your adolescent needs to know that if he feels anxious, unsafe or out of his depth, whatever the time of day or night and wherever he may be, he can call on you for help and you will unquestioningly come to his rescue – and that there will be no recriminations afterwards. We all make errors of judgement from time to time, and it is better that our children feel able to admit this to us and ask for our help than that they struggle on, suffering possibly danger-ous consequences, because they are too scared or embarrassed to admit their mistake.

Dealing with mistakes constructively

If we want our children to be able to come to us for help when they need it, to tell us their worries and ask our advice, the way we handle their inevitable mistakes is all-important.

When we find that our children have done something that we, and possibly they, would rather they had not done, how should we react?

- Get the facts straight first. Raise the matter courteously and without accusations, ask questions calmly and with an open mind, and listen to your child's answers.
- Don't overreact, and ask yourself calmly how important this issue really is. If necessary, postpone discussion until you have had a chance to think and talk things over.
- Help him to understand the consequences of his actions, both for himself and others.
- Even if he has behaved very badly, make it clear that you are upset about what he has done – but that you still love him, and have faith in him to do better next time.
- Don't protect your child from all the consequences of his mistakes, or leap to his defence even when he is clearly in the wrong. Acknowledging the need for rules and taking responsibility for one's own actions is an essential part of living in a civilized society.
- Be glad that your child is making his mistakes while you're still around and able to help him limit the damage and to learn from them.

Learning to handle money

Parents often complain about their teenagers' apparent belief that money 'grows on trees', but we cannot expect our children to understand the finite nature of their parents' income without a bit of firsthand experience of budgeting for themselves. Even very young children can be given a small quantity of money and helped to work out what it will buy. Making choices about what they *really* want, spending the money, and then realizing that they haven't got it to spend again – all this helps them to understand why you say that they can't have the expensive trainers they want because the money is needed to pay the gas bill.

Bank accounts

You can open a bank or building society account in your child's name no matter how young he is, but from the age of about 11 or 12 it is possible for your child to open an account in his own name, for which he is the signatory and can carry a cash card. These young people's accounts will not allow the account holder to overdraw, so there is no chance of his running up debts. Seeing his money accumulate (or disappear) will encourage your teenager to save, and he is more likely to think twice about spending his savings if he has to make a withdrawal first. As he gets older and starts to take on holiday jobs for which he may be paid by cheque or bank transfer, a bank account will be essential.

Try not to interfere with your teenager's spending too much. He is bound to make a few mistakes, but he will learn by them – and it's better to make such mistakes now than later, when his increased spending power may make them more expensive.

Allowances

Even before your child becomes an adolescent, you will probably be faced with a request for regular pocket money. There are at least three basic schools of thought on what sort of allowance children should get:

- A regular allowance, which they are free to spend on anything they like.
- A regular allowance, from which they are expected to pay for certain items, from outings and presents for friends, to clothing and school books.
- Nothing – children are entitled to two things from their parents: love and having their basic needs (food, shelter, basic clothing, etc.) met. Beyond this, everything has to be earned.

This third approach probably teaches children most about responsibility and the value of money, although it does require rather more input from parents than the other two – giving a teenager a job to do can be a good deal more time-consuming than doing it yourself.

Whatever their source, teenagers' allowances should be their own, to spend as they wish. If they have their hearts set on a big purchase, you can encourage them to save towards it by offering to contribute once they get beyond a certain amount, and there is no harm in rewarding a good school report or exam success with a gift of money – this, too, has been earned.

Savings

As well as a 'current' bank or building society account from which they can withdraw spending money as they need it, it is a good idea to establish a savings account for your child, in which money can be saved long term for, say, their first car. If you open such an account in your child's name, but with yourself as signatory, you can make a point of handing it over to him when he comes of age, gets his first job, or at some other milestone in his life. Relatives often welcome the chance to contribute to long-term savings on birthdays, and he may even decide to pay some money into it himself, once he understands the interest rate benefits of a long-term savings account. The main thing is to establish the idea of long-term savings, and the very tangible benefit he will derive from them. If you are saving for your adolescent's university fees, or even paying a mortgage, make sure that he knows about it, and understands the impact it has on your income as a family – all this will help him to grasp the importance of thinking long term where finance is concerned.

Leaving home

Anyone over the age of 16 is entitled in law to leave home and live independently of their parents. In practice, most young people continue to live with and be financially dependent on their parents into their late teens or twenties, even if they are away at university during term time.

The awful irony, for parents, is that they spend many, many years looking after a demanding, dependent baby, then an exhausting, expensive child, followed by a testing, tormented teenager – and then, just as he finally begins to turn into the helpful, mature, friendly, caring young adult we always hoped he would be, he ups and leaves home! It can be very difficult to see your child, particularly your first child, leave home, and in some cases our worries turn out to be justified:

> Jenny did well at school – she was self-motivated, worked hard, got good A-level results, and a place at the university of her choice. I wasn't unduly worried when I left her in her new room on the campus, but it just didn't work out. She was dreadfully homesick, she couldn't cope with the lack of supervision on her English course, and found it very hard to organize her study effectively. She didn't like life in student accommodation, and couldn't handle the pressure of shopping for herself and getting her own meals. She was increasingly miserable, and in the end she came home for a weekend and just didn't go back. I wish that we'd prepared her better for life away from home – I'm sure she would have coped with the course if she'd had more experience of looking after herself.

One solution to the problems caused by the huge leap between school and university life is the gap year. This is your child's chance to practise the skills she will need when she is living away from home in halls or privately rented accommodation, and you can help her to do so by gradually requiring her to take responsibility for her own washing, some of her own and the family's meals, shopping and travel arrangements. If she can find paid work, so much the better – this will be the last time she has any disposable income to speak of for at least three years and she can stock up on clothes, CDs, etc. – but, if not, it is important that this year is not wasted in getting up late and 'hanging out'. Encourage your adolescent to use the time doing voluntary work or pursuing an activity relevant to her university course, and pulling her weight at home too!

Runaways

Occasionally, in an effort to escape family or school problems or in an attempt to find a completely different way of life, teenagers run away from home. This may come as a complete surprise to their parents, who may not have realized that there was anything seriously wrong. If your child runs away, there are two vitally important things to remember when she returns, or when you find her:

- Make it absolutely clear to your child that she is still loved and welcome in the family home.
- Focus on the problems that made your child run away in the first place, and seek help for both yourselves and your child from counselling and mediation services, through your GP, or the contacts in the Useful Addresses at the back of this book.

Although you will naturally be angry or hurt, try to handle the situation in a constructive way. It is important that your child is not made to feel that she had burned her bridges, but is still welcome and safe at home with you.

Rebellion

We want our children to resist peer pressure when it comes to bad or dangerous behaviour; we hope that they will grow up with the courage of their convictions and faith in their own judgement – and we must accept that this may sometimes involve their going against our wishes and questioning authority. Sue recalls the day her daughter, Rachel, came home from school with some surprising news:

> She was one of a group of pupils who had achieved top grades in their GCSEs, and the school had arranged for their photograph to be taken for the local paper. Rachel had been unenthusiastic about the photo, but I'd brushed her reluctance aside as being undue modesty. When she got home I

asked her how the photo had gone, and she told me that she'd refused to take part. She said that there were lots of people in her year who had worked much harder than she had and got good results, and it wasn't fair that she should get her picture in the paper and they should get no recognition at all.

At first, I was just dreadfully disappointed that she'd missed this opportunity, then I was worried about her having flouted the school's authority. That only lasted a few minutes, though – before long it dawned on me that this was just the sort of adult responsibility I'd always hoped she'd take for her life. She saw something that she felt was wrong, and she challenged it – and authority and peer pressure didn't stop her from doing so. If more people were like that, there'd be a lot less wrong in the world. I also realized that, if I was really honest, my disappointment was mostly for myself; it would have been nice to see her in the paper, and my friends would have been terribly impressed. It had never been important to her at all.

What our children really need from us – the single most powerful aid to keeping them safe through the difficult teenage years and into adulthood – is a sense of their own worth. In order to make decisions that protect them from the worst of the dangers that life has to offer, they must first feel that they are worth protecting. For all of us, our feeling of self-worth is based upon a good, close relationship during childhood with parents who love us unconditionally for who we are – they may dislike some of the things we do or the way we behave at times, but never leave us in any doubt that they still love us. Come the upheaval of adolescence, this unconditional love gives the teenager an anchor that will prevent him from being swept away by confused emotions and conflicting demands, and enable him to return to a happy, adult relationship with his family when the process of establishing his independence is complete.

9
Family Life

Teenagers are so bound up in finding out about their new, adolescent selves that it amounts, at times, to self-obsession. This can be maddening for the rest of the family. They spend hours in front of the mirror, trying on clothes or doing and redoing make-up; they propound their own needs at every possible opportunity, apparently failing completely to recognize that anyone else has any; they ruthlessly crush their siblings while being exaggeratedly faithful to their friends.

At times teenagers can be completely oblivious of the power they have to madden and distress those around them, as they practise their newly developed powers of sarcasm and criticism indiscriminately on the rest of the family. Withering looks, sneering remarks, brooding silences and door-slamming all become a part of everyday life as the adolescent uses his emerging powers of critical appraisal to find fault with and reject the human failings of parents, teachers and all those he once looked up to and idealized. It can all be very, very nasty indeed. What almost makes it more difficult is the fact that, every now and then, there are glimpses of another, nicer person – the uncomplicated, loving child that we feel we have lost or the balanced, friendly adult she will become. It can be a very hard time for parents, but we shouldn't take it personally, however personally it seems to be intended.

Family activities

As teenagers create the space around themselves in which to grow up and become independent of their family, they inevitably begin to spend more time alone in their rooms, or talking on the telephone to their friends. Family activities that would once have delighted them are now rejected contemptuously as 'boring', and visits to relatives are greeted with rolled eyes and protestations of 'Do I have to go?' Holidays – days or weeks at a time spent in close contact with the family and away from all-important friends – can arouse out-and-out rebellion. All this can feel, especially when parents are tired or stressed, like a personal rejection; suddenly the child who vied constantly with siblings for your time, who was so eager for your attention and approval, would rather listen to tuneless music in a rubbish tip of a bedroom than sit in a warm, comfortable living room with you. It's easy to become angry.

If you drag him along on family outings, he may sulk, gripe and make everyone's experience of their day out as miserable as possible. Simply leaving him at home while everyone else goes out together, however, isn't without its own problems. Your teenager, especially in his early teenage years, still needs to feel a valued and loved part of your family – valued for the person he is and is becoming, not for the child he feels he no longer is. Excluding him from family activities, even though he makes it very clear that he doesn't want to take part, is bound eventually to make him feel rejected and misunderstood – so how can you make family activities more attractive to your teenager?

- Choose activities that have something to offer to teenagers, as well as to younger and older members of the family, and allow your adolescent to take part in activities that younger family members wouldn't enjoy. The larger theme parks usually cater for all ages.
- Encourage your teenager to bring a friend along. Being with someone of their own age can transform even their disdainful mockery of the outing into an enjoyable experience for an adolescent.
- Let your teenager choose some outings for himself, and leave younger children at home occasionally, thus sharing a more grown-up experience with your adolescent – perhaps an age-restricted film or a meal in a restaurant. She will appreciate being acknowledged and treated as a young adult.

Things get a bit more difficult when it comes to 'duty' visits to relatives. It is often hard for the teenager to understand why he should face a dreary afternoon at Granny's house; Granny still insists on treating him like a child, invading his personal space with hugs and kisses, and offering him orange squash when he would rather have coffee. Relatives may talk about him in his presence as though he were not there, there is nothing to do and, worst of all, he is out of contact with his all-important friends. He hasn't yet developed the empathy or the sense of responsibility for the feelings of others to appreciate and value what the visit will mean to Granny.

It is not unreasonable to expect your teenager to take on some responsibility towards members of the extended family, but there are ways in which we can make this easier for them:

- Understand and acknowledge that they find these visits difficult and irksome.
- Discuss with them the reasons for the visits, and help them to see the situation from Granny's point of view. Put the visit in the perspective of Granny's lifetime of interest and concern for their welfare and happiness, and the importance to her of the visit.
- Find ways together of making the visit as easy as possible. Perhaps he could take along a book or a Gameboy, to fall back on when he has done his duty and Granny's interest has turned to others in the family.

Ask him what he doesn't like about going to Granny's house, and agree to try and change things that can be changed. You could, for instance, explain privately to Granny that your son is growing up and becoming more self-conscious, and that hugs and kisses, or being talked about in his presence, make him uncomfortable. Could she please try to treat him more like a young adult than a child? Would she mind if he watched his favourite television programme at her house?

Find things that he can do for Granny, in his new role as a young adult, while he's there. Could he walk to the local shop and get some groceries? Could he shift a piece of furniture that's too heavy for her, or hack back the weeds in her garden? A job that makes him feel appreciated and acknowledges his ability to take responsibility will make the experience a more positive one for him (even if you have to offer to pay him for it later).

Give him plenty of notice before visits, and be willing to negotiate. Perhaps he need not come on every visit, if he makes the most of the times he is there to make Granny feel appreciated. If you agree that he can miss a visit, you can come up between you with an excuse that will not make Granny feel rejected.

Older teenagers might prefer to visit independently from time to time, if it is possible for them to get there under their own steam.

Siblings

We may manage to be broad-shouldered in our own dealings with our teenagers' sarcasm and criticism, but many of us are pushed over the edge into righteous fury when they pick on their younger siblings – and teenagers can be truly vicious in this respect:

> Imogen is five years older than her little brother, Christopher, and there has always been a bit of friction between them, but since she turned 13 things have really got out of hand. She never addresses a civil word to him; every time he opens his mouth she contradicts him in viciously sarcastic tones, she pokes fun at everything he does, and she'll even push or barge into him when she thinks I'm not looking, and swear blind that she hasn't done it. I have explained to her over and over again that what she's doing amounts to bullying, and that she could do his self-confidence serious, long-term harm if she carries on as she does, but she just says that he's 'annoying' and he 'winds her up'. I just don't know what to do about it.

This is not an uncommon scenario, but a very distressing one for all concerned. Often a real vicious circle is set up, with the teenager goading the younger child, the parent jumping in to protect him, the teenager feeling unjustly penalized and blaming the younger child, and the whole cycle starting again. Sooner or later, the parent starts to jump in even before the teenager has struck, the younger child starts to make the most of his immunity from blame, and begins to wind the teenager up for real, and the whole thing escalates into full-scale war.

You can't make your children love one another, although it is surprising how protective even the most abrasive teenager can be of her kid brother if someone from outside the family threatens him. There are ways to defuse the friction between siblings, however:

- Make it possible for your teenager to escape from the family by making her bedroom a pleasant place to be – warmth, comfortable seating, television, radio or CD player all help, and it must be understood by all that no one can enter without invitation.
- Make clear, simple rules about bullying behaviour – no hitting or pushing, no taking of possessions, etc., and apply them with a completely even hand to everyone in the family.
- Listen to each child's complaints about the other's behaviour, and help them to find better ways of coping with it.
- Explain carefully to your younger child that teenagers have a lot to cope with, and that it often makes them bad tempered. He needs to know that much of his older sibling's behaviour is not his fault, or indeed anything much to do with him at all. He also, however, needs to be helped to avoid making matters worse.

Do as I say, not as I do

During their childhood, we may have told our offspring how a child should behave, but we have shown them how an adult behaves. If we have been generally courteous, respectful of the rights and feelings of others (including our children), honest, hardworking and conscientious, then, although they may rebel

93

against our values for a time, their observations of adulthood will have become part of their internal template for life. The trouble is that our shortcomings will have been soaked up and internalized just as readily as our virtues, and if we have treated our family in an overbearing, thoughtless, disrespectful way, we should not be surprised if our children see this as an adult way to behave, and follow suit.

During adolescence, we cannot expect to receive respect from our teenagers if we do not give it, and because we are the ones with the life experience, it is often up to us to grit our teeth and persevere in our reasonable treatment of our children, even when they are at their most unreasonable. If we can't maintain our principles in the face of turmoil, upset and confusion, how can we expect them to?

Family meetings

One effective way of ensuring that everyone in the family has a voice is to hold a regular or occasional 'family meeting'. As teenagers mature, it becomes necessary to change family rules and expectations to take account of their increasing maturity, but proposals for change tend to come about as the result of a disagreement or transgression, when tempers are short and defences are up. Where there is a meeting on the horizon, discussion can be deferred until then, and everyone has the chance to calm down, marshal their arguments, and often to modify their views before the issue is debated.

The family meeting is not a suitable forum for every issue – some boil down to parental responsibility and/or money, and while these may be discussed and views tabled, parents have to have the final say. Such meetings do, however, deal very effectively with many areas of conflict – who should do what around the house, how time on the computer should be allocated, what considerations should be shown for the privacy of other family members, and so on. When expectations have to be renegotiated for older children, meetings can enable both the adolescent and others in the family to see and understand the need both for having the rules, and for changing them as circumstances change.

Chores

It would be nice to think that, as they grew up, our children would gradually assume responsibility for some of the dozens of boring, repetitive household chores that have to be done every day, just to keep the wheels of family life turning. Some families manage this, but many find it an uphill struggle:

> I just find that it's far, far easier for me simply to get on and do the washing up, or take out the rubbish, myself than to cajole a reluctant and resentful teenager into doing it. I used to worry about this, but then, when my older two children went off to university and returned home during the holidays, I noticed a dramatic change. Suddenly they volunteered to do the washing up without being asked – not only that, they insisted on doing it in their own, special way. My son offered to carry shopping for me, my daughter made me cups of tea. I realized that all the time and energy, all the resentment and reproach, could have been avoided after all. In a few short weeks of looking after themselves and, more importantly, experiencing the consequences of *not* looking after them- selves, they had learned what all my cajoling couldn't teach them.

Most young people will eventually learn to look after them- selves, so is it really worth insisting that your teenager pulls his weight? Since taking responsibility contributes to self-esteem, it would seem so – as long as you set each child a few, simple chores, of which they can easily see the benefit to themselves and which fall well within their capabilities. Here are some examples that I have used with my own four children:

- They must put their clothes out for washing when asked, or they will not have clean clothes to wear.

- If they cook for themselves, they must put away the ingredients after use and wash up utensils. If they don't, I won't let them do it the next time they ask.
- They must turn off lights and the television when they are not in use, because if they don't, the money wasted will not be available for the purchase of their clothes and shoes.
- They must tidy away after themselves, and anything they leave lying around will be deposited in their rooms for them to sort out.

One way of encouraging teenagers to take on household and garden chores is to offer payment, and this can take the place of pocket money; of course, they must do a good job if they want to get paid. In this arrangement, everyone benefits – you get the jobs done, they feel appreciated and earn pocket money, and the atmosphere at home is immeasurably sweeter for the absence of strife over chores not done and burdens resented.

Beyond the family

As children enter adolescence, their curiosity about the world outside the family and those who populate it begins to grow. They start to see the world and the future as something more relevant to them, and as they watch the news on television or read about it in the press, they begin to identify with the plight of those involved.

Struggling still to make sense of their own lives and emotions, teenagers will often form extremely idealistic and inflexible views over a great range of issues; they may also feel let down by parents who don't fall in with their views of right and wrong, and become intensely critical of their perceived shortcomings. Judith, the mother of two grown-up and one teenage child, has come in for her share of criticism:

I remember with great shame and embarrassment my own arguments with my father, who was a parachute pathfinder in the Second World War. Convinced that war was absolutely wrong under all circumstances, I was vociferously critical of his part in it; after all, I reasoned, he could have become a conscientious objector – he didn't have to go out and kill people. Later, with an adult understanding of what the Second World War was all about, and of what it cost men like my father to risk their lives and to see their comrades and, in my father's case, his beloved younger brother, fall around them, I realized how little understanding I had possessed, at 14, of the impossible choices that adults have to make in life, and was and am amazed at my father's calmness in the face of my tirades. The point is, though, that nothing he could have said then would have given me that understanding – I came to it in my own time. When my teenagers have expounded what appear, to an adult, to be ludicrously simplistic views of complex issues, I have reminded myself of my own understanding at 14, and simply tried to explain a little of the complexity to them. They have a right to their views, and to change them as maturity and understanding grows.

Sometimes, teenagers feel strongly that they want to *do* something about the issues they care about. For parents who are pouring all their energies into work and family and have none left over for pursuing causes, this may seem just a bit too much like hard work, and their teenagers may get a lukewarm response. The feeling that they can actually do something to make the world a bit better can bring such benefits to young people, though, that it really is worth encouraging them to turn their idealism into action. Whether this means joining Greenpeace or helping to clear a local canal, properly constituted and supervised groups and activities that benefit others can give adolescents a sense of belonging; of being valuable and valued, and of having the power to change things for the better.

10
Sex and Sexuality

Puberty transforms our children into sexual beings. In physical terms, they are capable of becoming parents from perhaps the age of 12 or 13, when girls' periods begin and boys start to produce sperm. Indeed, a small minority of adolescents do become parents – here in the United Kingdom we have the highest teenage pregnancy rate in Western Europe. However, the fact that most teenagers don't become parents in their early teens is not simply a testament to the strength of society's or their parents' conditioning.

Prior to puberty, boys and girls interact together quite freely, but as adolescence approaches there is a distinct split between the sexes, with friendships across gender boundaries becoming far less common – each sex sees the other as fundamentally different and somehow mysterious, and antagonism between boys and girls becomes the rule. Before they can bridge this gap and form relationships with a member of the opposite sex, teenagers must find a whole new way of relating to one another, and for most it takes time and a good deal of cautious experimentation before they feel ready to have their first boyfriend/girlfriend relationship, let alone progress to sex itself.

Young teenagers are often tongue-tied and awkward around members of the opposite sex, although they are keenly interested in theory, and will probably start by worshipping the object of their interest from afar, whether it be a pop idol or a classmate. Each sex will discuss the other endlessly, but contact will be minimal, and even when they do go on their first date, very little that is overtly sexual is likely to happen.

We are unique among mammals in consciously controlling our own fertility, and we are able to do so only because our large and highly developed brains are capable of overriding our natural urge to reproduce. In order to exert this control over our lives, we need knowledge – we need to understand the reproductive process, and to be aware that there are options.

Children in our society are constantly bombarded with

information about sex, but much of it is intended to entertain or titillate, and can leave them confused and anxious about the whole business of sexual relationships and what they might mean in their own lives. It is vital that children are provided with straightforward, balanced information from a very early age – long before the physical and emotional changes of adolescence make it both essential for their understanding of those changes and also more difficult to talk about because it affects them so personally.

All children will learn about sex and relationships at school, as part of both the Science and the Personal Social and Health Education (PSHE) curricula. What is taught in science lessons is laid down by the National Curriculum, but the content of PSHE lessons is determined by the school's staff and governors. Each school must have a written Sex and Relationship Education (SRE) policy, which will describe the way in which sex and relationships will be taught there. When this policy is changed, the school is expected to ask parents' views on the proposed changes, and parents should also be informed when SRE is going to take place, and told what their children will be learning. You can ask to see the school's SRE policy, and you are free to withdraw your child from the SRE lessons that take place as part of the PSHE curriculum, if you wish, but not from those that form part of the compulsory science curriculum (see below).

What is 'Sex and Relationship Education'?

SRE is defined by the DfES as 'lifelong learning about physical and moral development'. It involves, the definition continues, 'teaching about sex, sexuality and sexual health, as well as the importance of stable and loving relationships, and of marriage for family life. It is not about the promotion of any particular sexual orientation or of sexual activity.' It is not clear how lifelong learning can be provided by schools, but the DfES produces guidelines on the teaching of SRE, advising schools on the topics that they should cover, as follows:

SRE in National Curriculum Science

Key Stage 2 (7–11 years)
Children in this age group will be taught:

- That animals, including humans, move, feed, grow, use their senses and reproduce.
- To recognize and name the main external parts of the human body.
- That humans can produce offspring and these grow into adults.
- To recognize similarities and differences between themselves and others and treat others with sensitivity.
- Life processes relevant to humans including nutrition, growth and reproduction.
- The main stages of the human life cycle.

Key Stage 3 (12–13 years)
This age group will study:

- The physical and emotional changes that take place during adolescence.
- The human reproductive cycle, including the menstrual cycle and fertilization.
- How the growth and reproduction of bacteria and the replication of viruses can affect human health.

Key Stage 4 (14–16 years)
These older teenagers will study:

- Hormonal control in humans, including the effects of sex hormones.
- Medical uses of hormones, including the control and promotion of fertility.
- How sex is determined in humans.

SRE in PSHE lessons

The content of PSHE lessons will vary from school to school, but will be laid out in a policy document that all parents are entitled to see. Many schools, for instance, will feel that leaving it until Key Stage 3 to talk to girls about menstruation as part of the science curriculum is unwise, as many girls start their periods earlier than this. Topics covered may include:

IN PRIMARY SCHOOLS:
- The physical and emotional effects of puberty.
- Menstruation.

IN SECONDARY SCHOOLS – THE ABOVE, PLUS:
- Assertiveness and negotiating skills to avoid exploitation, and resist pressure to take part in risky behaviour.
- Contraception. For those pupils who ask for help in this area, this may include information on where to get advice on, and the availability of, the various methods of contraception.
- Abortion.
- Safe sex, HIV, AIDS and sexually transmitted diseases.

The issues covered in PSHE (and the way in which they are taught) will vary, with schools that have a strongly religious ethos, for instance, approaching the issue of abortion in a different way from schools that have no connection with a particular faith. Teachers should guide discussions sensitively, working with the class to set out ground rules that avoid embarrassment or the pressure to contribute.

What can parents do?

Although the facts will be covered at school, many feel that SRE is too little, too late, and too focused on the biological aspects of sex and relationships at the expense of emotional issues. Children still need to put their sexual and relationship development in the context of their own life and family. Much of their early knowledge and understanding of relationships will come from observation of their parents, and it will help our children if, from the earliest days, we talk about sex and relationships in terms that they can understand. The many available books dealing with these subjects, designed to be read by parents with their children, can be very helpful in raising questions and providing suitably targeted answers.

Some parents find it hard to talk to their teenagers about sex and sexual development without embarrassment, and it has to be said that many teenagers feel the same. If we have spoken openly about sex with our younger children, it feels natural to continue to do so when they become adolescents, but often parents put off talking about sex with their children until they 'need to know', and then find that it is too late; once the effects of puberty have kicked in, the general disruption of the parent/child relationship, coupled with the adolescent's new thirst for privacy and embarrassment about his body and emotions, may make him unwilling to take part in discussions. All is not lost, though:

- Even if you can't easily talk with your child, you can provide him with information in the form of books and pamphlets – and via internet sites, though these need careful selection.
- Take an interest in his SRE lessons at school, and ask him questions about the sessions and his views on the issues raised (allowing that he may not always want to respond).
- Take the opportunity to discuss with your child any relevant issues raised by television programmes or events in the lives of your family or friends. Make these discussions a part of everyday life, rather than a lecture.
- Talk about the emotional issues surrounding sex and relationships, and share experiences from your own teenage years, even if you or he don't feel comfortable talking about the biological details.
- Listen to your child's questions and concerns, being sensitive to the unspoken questions 'between the lines', and answer them as fully as you can, or direct him to sources of further information. When it comes to learning about sex and relationships, the emotional context is just as important as his new-found factual knowledge, and only you can know your child well enough to answer his unspoken as well as his spoken questions.

Emotions and sex

For humans, sex is not just a physical activity. There are very few people who can engage sexually with another individual without investing a good deal of emotion in the relationship, even if it is a casual one; joy, disgust, acceptance, rejection, affirmation, humiliation – we open ourselves up to a host of powerful feelings when we have a sexual encounter, and even experienced adults have difficulty sometimes in handling the consequences. Teenagers experiencing the power of these feelings for the first time can be overwhelmed, and feel confused and out of control.

As parents, we cannot entirely protect our children from difficult or painful situations. We can, however, help them to develop the understanding and skills necessary both to consider others and look after themselves. Even before puberty begins, we can talk with them about the things we feel are important in relationships – for instance:

- Trust and communication.
- Consideration for the feelings and needs of others.
- Ways of resolving arguments and setting boundaries.

As sexual maturity approaches, we need to talk to our teenager about more specific aspects of sexual relationships. We may want to discuss morality, and this is not just about any religious views we may hold – it's about being responsible in our dealings with others. Among the topics we could discuss are:

- Not having sex unless both partners are ready.
- Considering the needs and feelings of sexual partners.
- Using contraception to avoid pregnancy.
- Avoiding sexually transmitted infections.
- Discussing honestly with partners the sort of relationship both want.

Just because a teenager can have sex legally, it doesn't necessarily follow that he will. In reality, the average age for first intercourse is probably about 17, with many waiting far longer than this before they feel ready to have sex for the first time. Teenagers' attitudes to sex may well be influenced by their gender, too:

- Boys are generally keen to be seen as sexually experienced by their peer group, and tend to play up their sexual encounters to their friends, or to invent them if they haven't had any. They may put pressure on girlfriends to have sex before they are ready, partly because their sexual needs are physically very pressing, and partly because they feel that they should lose their virginity as soon as possible.
- Girls are more likely to want to delay having sex until they feel ready, or until they meet someone with whom they feel comfortable and safe. The girl who sleeps with lots of boys is likely to be seen as a 'slag' by her peer group and, ironically, by the boys themselves.

Sex is so prevalent in films and on television, in advertising and in magazines aimed at the teenage market, that teenagers may feel that everyone is having sex but them. Surveys clearly show that this is not true, and it would be helpful to many teenagers to know this. Both boys and girls need help in finding ways of listening to their own needs, and resisting the pressure to have sex before they are ready.

Dating

At first, the young teenager often falls in love from a distance – sometimes with someone she has next to no chance of ever meeting, let alone forming a relationship with. The feelings are very real, however, and can amount almost to obsession. Sooner or later, however, most teenagers will embark (tentatively at first) on a real relationship. This process is fraught with challenges and obstacles – the initial expression of interest, holding hands for the first time, what to do on a date, how to kiss properly – any one of which might result in rejection, embarrassment or humiliation for either or both partners. Dave remembers his first date only too clearly:

I took a girl from school to the local folk club. We went on a bus and had to walk the last mile over fields in the dark, arriving very late. Throughout the whole evening, I don't think that we exchanged more than twenty words or so, we were both so tense and embarrassed. When it was over, we hitchhiked back to town, where she missed the last train and I had to put her in a taxi, spending my life savings. Although we had hardly spoken, I summoned up the courage to kiss her, my hands wandered a little, and she asked me what I thought I was doing, to which there was no reply. Even thinking about it now makes me go cold. And of course the whole of the sixth form knew every detail the next day. It was months before I plucked up the courage to ask anyone out again.

Despite the angst, teenagers do fall in love, and often very deeply. Any suggestion that this is simply 'puppy love' will, quite reasonably, make them very angry and unhappy indeed. Sometimes the almost overwhelming new emotions they are experiencing make it very hard for the adolescent to concentrate on anything else at all, and schoolwork and after-school interests may suffer.

The end of a relationship can cause enormous distress that persists sometimes for many months, and in extreme cases can cause real depression and even suicidal thoughts. There is nothing 'put on' or childish about these emotions – they are real and deeply felt, and your child will need your support and understanding in learning to cope with them. Without any previous experience of relationship problems, the teenager is not able to console himself with the thought that, however unhappy he feels at the moment, he will eventually get over it and move on to other relationships.

In reality, it is only in the case of the very young teenager that parents have much control over their relationships with the opposite sex. Once our adolescents are away from direct parental supervision, we have to accept that it is they, not we, who are responsible for their welfare. We can explain the facts of life, we can talk with them about the physical and emotional consequences of their behaviour, we can do our best to see that they believe in themselves and their own worth enough to look after themselves, but in the end it's down to them. How can we help them, therefore, with some of the big issues that sex and sexuality throw up?

Sexual orientation

Some parents worry that their child, as he passes through adolescence, may form a sexual attachment to a person of the same sex. This worry may be triggered or fed by behaviour in their child that parents think of as being characteristic of the opposite sex, by close same-sex friendships, or by their suspicions about the company their child keeps.

The reasons for some individuals being romantically, physically, emotionally and sexually attracted to members of the same sex (homosexuality) or both sexes (bisexuality) are not clearly understood. What is certain is that homosexuality is not anyone's 'fault', and neither is sexual orientation a matter of choice for the individual concerned.

Some people are never attracted to the opposite sex at all, but find themselves, at the time when they are becoming sexually aware, attracted solely to members of their own sex. Sometimes things are not so straightforward; it is normal for some adolescents to be unsure of their sexual orientation, and to experiment with same-sex and heterosexual relationships – there are many things that they are unsure of at this stage – but this is a process of discovery, not of determination. For a few people, sexual orientation may never be clear-cut, and they may have relationships with both sexes at different points during their life.

Homosexual relationships, just like the heterosexual sort, come in all varieties from the loving and stable, to the casual and destructive. Why, then, does the idea that their child may be attracted to members of the same sex fill some parents with anxiety? They may feel that:

- Homosexuality still carries some stigma, and their child will be hurt or disadvantaged by it.
- Their cherished vision of the future as grandparents of a standard, 2.4-child family is lost (although gay couples do, increasingly, become parents).
- They have failed, both in their own eyes and those of others, as parents.
- They are responsible for the homosexuality, and have let their child down.

Some parents cope constructively with these fears, but others become angry or disappointed with their child, blaming him for their distress and pressuring him to change. Because sexual orientation is something that we have no control over, this leaves the teenager with only two options – to try to live a life he knows he is not right for, or to cut his parents off entirely from the part of his life that they cannot accept (or, often more easily, his life as a whole).

What should you do if you think your child might be gay?

Parents may have suspected for some time that their child is attracted to the same sex, but sometimes the revelation, whether it comes from the child or is discovered by chance, is totally unexpected and profoundly shocking. In either case, it is important that parents do not overreact. Remember that:

- Sexual orientation is not a matter of choice.
- Your child cannot change his sexual orientation, and you certainly cannot make him.
- Sexual orientation is not an illness, and there is no 'cure' for homosexuality or bisexuality.
- Your child needs your unconditional love and support through his teenage years.
- He will have additional social pressures to cope with, and needs you to stand by him.

- The important thing is that his relationships are safe.
- In telling you about his sexual orientation, your child has placed great trust and confidence in you. He needs you to show him the same respect.

Homosexuality raises questions about sex and relationships that are not as readily answered by the information available to teenagers as are those relating to heterosexual relationships. There are, however, many sources of information for young people who are, or think they may be, gay, and some are listed in Useful Addresses at the back of this book. One of the constructive things that parents can do for their children is to help them find out as much as they can about being gay in a largely 'straight' society, and to arrive themselves at an understanding of the way that homosexuality can affect their child's life.

Try to avoid endless questions about why your child may be homosexual. It doesn't matter – like the rest of his personality, it is a small part of the whole person you love.

Sexual exploitation

There can be few parents, nowadays, who do not teach their children about 'stranger danger'. We are all well aware of the activities of paedophiles, and most of us take steps to protect our young children from sexual abuse. When they become teenagers, things become far more complicated. Now our children are sexual beings with drives of their own – and the distinction between abuser and sexual partner is not so clear-cut, and we find ourselves worrying not just about the situations they may find themselves in, but about the decisions they may make. How can we protect them from sexual abuse or exploitation by others who are older, more experienced, or just more cynical and self-seeking than themselves?

In their early teens, while we still have a degree of control over their lives, we can make sure that our children keep company largely with others of their own age; we can allow them to stay only in the houses of children whose parents we know and trust; we can talk and listen to our children, and pick up the signs of any discomfort they feel about individuals they come into contact with – friends' older siblings, sports coaches, youth group leaders and so on – and listen to what other parents have to say about them. As they become older, however, and start to live part of their lives away from our gaze and on their own terms, they will need to acquire some of the skills of adult relationships in order to keep themselves physically and emotionally safe:

- Empathy – the ability to gauge what others are feeling.
- Assertiveness.
- Negotiation skills.
- Avoidance of situations in which they are out of control.
- Confidence and self-respect.

These skills, which are learned within the family and built on by positive experiences outside the home, protect our children not only from abuse, but from abusing others too. The ability to appreciate and respect the feelings of others and the confidence to accept their rejection without anger or denial all help to ensure that we treat teenagers with the consideration and respect with which we would like to be treated ourselves.

Sex and the law

The law offers some protection against the abuse of children and adolescents by older individuals, though it does vary depending on gender:

- A man or boy over the age of ten can be prosecuted for unlawful sexual intercourse with a girl under the age of 16, even if she gives her consent.
- A woman or girl cannot be prosecuted for unlawful sexual intercourse, but can be prosecuted for indecent assault or gross indecency if she has sex with a boy under the age of 16, even if he gives his consent. Such prosecutions are rare.

- A woman who has a lesbian relationship with a girl who is under 16 may be charged with indecent assault, although again such prosecutions are rare.
- It is illegal for a man who is under 18 to have a homosexual relationship. Under-16s who engage in homosexual activity together can be charged with indecent assault (because under-16s cannot give consent).
- Even where those involved are of the age of consent, anyone forcing a partner to take part in sexual intercourse without their consent can be liable to prosecution.

Contraception

Around 100,000 teenage girls in the United Kingdom become pregnant every year, with around 10 per cent of that number being under 16 when they conceive. Many choose to have a termination, some keep their baby, and a few put their child up for adoption, but in any case their life is changed for ever. Most of us would rather that this didn't happen to our teenage daughters – and that our teenage sons didn't father a child outside a stable, enduring relationship with the mother – but the fact is that the average age for having sex for the first time in this country is thought to be 17, and many teenagers much younger than this will have run the risk of pregnancy by having unprotected sex.

We may well hope, as parents, that our children delay their first experience of intercourse until they are older than this, and many do; self-esteem and a sense of responsibility help to ensure this. We have to accept, though, that a great many teenagers will have sex, regardless of our views. If and when they do, it is vitally important that they practise safe sex, in terms both of contraception and the avoidance of sexually transmitted disease.

Despite the inclusion of SRE on the school curriculum, there is evidence of an alarming lack of knowledge among teenagers concerning contraception. In a recent survey, doctors reported a range of bizarre myths, gleaned from their interviews with teenage patients. Having sex in the bath, keeping your eyes closed, and drinking a lot of alcohol were advanced, among others, as effective contraceptive methods. How can these beliefs persist when so much is done to educate children about sex? Perhaps the rejection by some teenagers of all the values and precepts of the older generation goes some way towards explaining this – many teenagers will give far more weight to something told to them by a friend, however unlikely it may seem, than to anything they are taught at school.

This resistance on the part of some children to anything that is perceived as 'education' makes it doubly important that they hear about important matters like sex and contraception from sources other than school. How much of this comes directly from you will depend on your relationship with your child, but don't be surprised if she doesn't want to talk to you about such intimate matters. Would you have been comfortable talking to your mum or dad about contraception? There are many sources of help and advice on sex and contraception for young people, however, and even if you can't easily talk to your child about these things, you can still collect leaflets for her to read, and make sure she knows where to go for help and can get there. If we feel that our child is not ready for sex, withholding information about contraception is not a way of preventing her from having sex – it simply ensures that if and when she does, she will run the risk of unplanned pregnancy and sexually transmitted infection.

Sources of help with regard to contraception

Teenage sex is often unplanned, and sometimes teenagers are too embarrassed to bring up the subject of contraception, or aren't sure whether they are at risk of pregnancy or not. In an emergency, two forms of contraception are available:

- Emergency hormonal contraception – the 'morning after' pill. This must be taken within 72 hours of intercourse.
- The intrauterine device (IUD) or coil. If inserted within five days of unprotected intercourse, it prevents pregnancy from

becoming established. In practice, this is seldom used in young girls.

It is important for teenagers to know that emergency contraception exists, and how to obtain it in these circumstances.

Many teenagers will need help in tackling the subject of contraception, and often they will need more help than you can give them, even if they are willing or able to discuss such intimate details of their sexual lives with you – and, for many, this will be unthinkable. So how and where can teenagers get contraceptive advice?

The family GP

The family doctor, who will know your child's medical and family background, is an obvious source of contraceptive advice for teenagers. If they wish, they can see the family GP without your knowledge, and it is legal in the United Kingdom for doctors to prescribe contraceptives confidentially to under-16s with or without their parents' permission, if they feel that they will have sex anyway, and there may be a risk of pregnancy, and if attempts to persuade children to confide in their parents have failed. For some teenagers, however, the embarrassment of talking about contraception to someone they may have known throughout their childhood may make it difficult to talk to their GP in this way. In some practices, a nurse will be available for contraceptive advice, and some teenagers may find her easier to talk to. Contraception is free through the NHS.

Family planning clinics

These are usually held in health centres or hospitals, and details of your nearest family planning clinic can be found in the telephone directory, or at the local health centre, hospital or health authority. Contraception here is free through the NHS.

Genitourinary medicine (GUM) and sexual health clinics

These specialize in sexually transmitted infections, but will also give contraceptive advice. You can get the number of a clinic in your area from the telephone directory (under GUM, STD, special or sexual health clinic), or from NHS Direct. Treatment is free, completely confidential, and open to people of any age or sexual orientation.

Services for young people

Many health authorities make special provision for young people, and details are available from the school nurse, the telephone directory and from the Family Planning Association (FPA) helpline or website (see Useful Addresses at the back of this book).

Pharmacies

Some pharmacists sell emergency contraceptive pills, and some can supply them free. In a few areas they are available free from certain supermarkets. Any pharmacist not providing this service will be able to tell you of one who does.

NHS walk-in centres

Some areas are covered by NHS walk-in centres, which are open long hours and over weekends and bank holidays. Most of these will be able to supply emergency contraceptive pills. Details of centres are available from NHS Direct (0845 4647), from the FPA, or from the government's website – www.doh.gov.uk/nhswalkincentres.

School nurse

Your child first meets the school nurse at primary school, and their relationship will continue into secondary school, where she will conduct some of their SRE sessions. You will have the opportunity to meet her yourself, with your child, when your child's regular development checks come round at 11 and 14. Most school nurses have a room in the school where children can drop in for a chat during the school day, and can advise on matters relating to sexual health, including contraception. These consultations will be confidential, although the school nurse may decide to inform parents or others if she thinks that the child is at risk.

Sexually transmitted infection (STI)

With rates of STI running at around 10 per cent among British teenagers, contracting one of these diseases is a far more common consequence of unprotected sex than pregnancy. Most can be treated easily and successfully if caught early enough, but some cannot, and some may have serious consequences for health and fertility if treatment is delayed. It is very important that teenagers understand the risk posed by STIs, and are aware of the steps they can take to avoid them.

Almost all STIs can be avoided by the use of condoms (male or female), and perhaps finding one in your teenager's pocket or bag should be an occasion for quiet relief rather than the shock it often causes. Not only could it protect your adolescent from unwanted pregnancy and disease – it doesn't even mean he is having sex. Many teenage boys carry them around 'just in case', and because it makes them feel grown up, and appear so in front of their mates. Rob, now the father of two grown-up children, remembers carrying a condom in his wallet as a 17-year-old:

> It was there for so long, untouched, that it left its imprint in the leather of my wallet. I'm not sure I'd really have known what to do with it, had the opportunity arisen, but you just had to have one – all my mates did too.

All teenagers need information about the risk of catching a STI, and sexually active teenagers need to be aware of signs that could indicate an infection, which include:

- Pain, swelling, itching or soreness of the sexual organs.
- Unusual discharge.
- Bleeding between periods.
- Lower abdominal pain.
- Pain when passing urine.
- Blisters or sores on the genitals.
- General flu-like symptoms.

Getting treatment for STIs

The family GP can provide treatment for STIs, usually in the form of a course of antibiotics, or it is possible to go straight to a sexual health or genitourinary medicine (GUM) clinic – sometimes listed under STD, VD, special or sexual health clinic in the telephone directory.

Human Immunodeficiency Virus (HIV) and Acquired Immune Deficiency Syndrome (AIDS)

Because they cannot be cured, HIV and AIDS are the most feared of the STIs, and there can be few parents who have not considered anxiously the possibility of their child becoming infected through early, ill-considered sexual activity.

Because of their immature grasp of the consequences of their actions, both for themselves and others, the risk of contracting HIV may seem remote and irrelevant to some teenagers, and this is one area where they cannot afford to learn from experience – but how real is the risk of contracting HIV in the United Kingdom from unprotected sex? The following facts (provided by the Terrence Higgins Trust, and current at the end of September 2002) may surprise those who believe that HIV is largely a disease of gay men and intravenous drug users:

- By the end of September 2002, 52,729 people in the United Kingdom had been diagnosed HIV positive since the disease was first recognized, and 12,504 people had been reported as dying with AIDS.
- Of these, 2,945 were recorded as newly diagnosed HIV positive in 2002 – just over 1,700 fewer than in 2001.
- It was estimated that, at the end of 2002, there were just over 41,000 people in the United Kingdom living with HIV, some of whom did not know that they had been infected.
- Some 45 per cent of cases overall had been diagnosed between the ages of 25 and 34, with none at all diagnosed in the 10–14 age group, and only 2 per cent between the ages of 15 and 19.

- Since 1999, the majority of infections have been heterosexually acquired and, of these, most were acquired abroad.
- There has been a decline in HIV infections associated with intravenous drug use, although a rise in the spread of the hepatitis virus infections by that route indicates that there is still a danger of further spread of HIV among drug users.

You can see from these figures that the risk of a teenager acquiring HIV through sex with someone in their peer group is actually quite low – much lower than the risk of contracting another, less intractable, STI – and could be avoided almost entirely through the adoption of safer sex. While not a reason for complacency, this should be some comfort to parents who worry constantly about the AIDS threat to their sexually active child.

11
Drugs, Alcohol and Smoking

One of the choices that teenagers face in their new life independent of their parents concerns their possible use of recreational drugs, including alcohol and tobacco. Every high street in the United Kingdom has its pub, tobacconist or off-licence, while the availability of low-priced, illegal drugs to children in ever-younger age groups has increased to such an extent that schools throughout the country are calling in police sniffer dogs to check their premises. No parent can afford to ignore the problem on the grounds that they believe their child will not come into contact with drugs or drug use. The factors that influence the teenager's decision to use or not to use drugs will include their knowledge of the substances themselves and the risks involved in their use, their own self-esteem, and the attitude and example of their parents where drug use is concerned.

You can help your child by finding out as much as you can about drugs, their use and misuse, and sharing this information with your teenager. It is important that you are prepared to talk honestly with her about drugs – she will know, or find out, if you are inventing or exaggerating the dangers involved, and scare tactics will simply lead her to reject everything that you have to say.

In this chapter you will find brief descriptions of the more commonly available recreational drugs, including alcohol and tobacco, which many people probably don't think of as drugs at all. Both alcohol and tobacco are dangerously addictive and frequently misused, however, and your child needs to be forewarned about the risks of using them just as much as about the more often stated dangers of illegal drugs. For sources of further information and support concerning drugs and drug abuse, see Useful Addresses at the back of this book.

Some of the dangers of recreational drug use relate to the method or circumstances of manufacture, supply and administration rather than to the drug itself, and injecting any drug is particularly dangerous. It is important that all teenagers understand the general risks of drug taking, which include:

- *Unsafe sex*
  Someone who is under the influence of drink or drugs may do, or be persuaded to do, things that they would avoid when sober.
- *Overdose*
  The user may take too much in one go, which can cause unexpected or damaging results.
- *Overuse*
  The user may indulge in use of the drug to the point where his ability to carry on a normal life is affected, and he may either fail to develop, or lose, the ability to cope with life in other ways. Some users will become addicted to some drugs.
- *Accident*
  Most drugs affect co-ordination and reaction time so that falls, or accidents when driving or operating machinery, become more likely.
- *Adulteration*
  Illicit drugs are not subject to the same controls as legitimate products, and may be impure or of unknown strength.
- *Mixing drugs*
  Taking more than one drug at a time, or even within several hours of each other, can change and increase their effects and the likelihood that they will do harm.
- *Deterioration in lifestyle*
  Habitual drug users may neglect their health, or spend so much money on drugs that they cannot afford to feed or house themselves properly.
- *Involvement in criminal activity*
  Possessing and dealing in many drugs are criminal offences. Heavy users may finance their habit by turning to crime or prostitution.
- *Dangers arising from injection*
  Whatever the drug used, injection introduces its own risks. The danger of overdose is increased; infection can occur as a

118

result of the use of non-sterile equipment, with serious diseases such as hepatitis and AIDS becoming a real risk where needles and syringes are shared. Poor injection technique and the injection of substances that are not prepared for that purpose, such as crushed tablets, can cause abscesses, gangrene and other serious problems.

As well as the general risks attached to the use of any drug, most drugs have their own, more specific risks or side-effects. A great variety of substances, both drugs that originally developed as medicines and substances that have no medical application, have been, and are, used recreationally, but the most commonly used recreational drugs – i.e. those that are most easily acquired and relatively cheap, and therefore most likely to be offered or available to teenagers – include:

Alcohol

The active ingredient of alcoholic drinks is ethyl alcohol, which is produced by fermenting grain, fruits and vegetables. At moderate doses (one or two pints of beer for most people), the user feels relaxed and sociable. Mental and physical functioning is reduced progressively depending on the amount of alcohol taken, and at higher doses the user becomes uncoordinated, with slurred speech, and may become emotional and/or aggressive. If drinking continues, double vision and loss of balance, and eventually unconsciousness, will result.

Tolerance to alcohol develops with repeated use, and the user will have to drink more and more to get the same effect. Physical and psychological dependence are very real dangers, and the regular and heavy drinker will experience withdrawal symptoms – including sweating, anxiety, trembling and delirium – if his supply of alcohol is stopped suddenly. Severe withdrawal can result in convulsions, coma and death.

Regular, heavy drinking can cause stomach, liver and brain damage. Because it has a high calorific content, drinking can lead to obesity and to dietary deficiencies (where a significant part of the calorific content of the user's diet is replaced by alcohol). The loss of self-control associated with alcohol use can lead to violence and relationship problems.

Tobacco

The active ingredient in tobacco is nicotine, a mild stimulant. When tobacco smoke is inhaled, nicotine is absorbed from the lungs into the bloodstream, rapidly reaching the brain.

The effects of tobacco smoke inhalation are almost immediate, and they build up during the smoking of each cigarette, declining rapidly after it is finished. Pulse rate and blood pressure increase, skin temperature is lowered, and appetite is reduced. The smoker feels alert and better able to concentrate, even if tired or bored, although someone new to smoking may simply feel dizzy and sick.

Tolerance to the effects of nicotine builds up rapidly, and dependency is very likely to develop, with most people who begin to smoke becoming regular users. Such users who try to stop smoking will feel jittery, irritable, depressed, and unable to concentrate, and it has been said by some people who have experienced both that smoking is harder to give up than heroin use.

Smoking is an extremely damaging habit. The risk of heart disease, thrombosis, bronchitis and other chest complaints, stroke, circulatory problems, ulcers and cancer of the mouth, throat and lungs are all increased; it is estimated that tobacco contributes to at least 100,000 premature deaths in the United Kingdom every year, and that a quarter of young male cigarette smokers will have their deaths hastened by the effects of tobacco use.

Solvents

Solvents are easily available over the counter in many forms, including glues, thinners, cleaning fluids and aerosols. Because they are so cheap and easy to get hold of, children and teenagers may be, and often are, tempted to experiment with them.

Glues (the most commonly misused solvents) are generally put into a plastic bag, and their vapours inhaled through the nose and mouth. Other substances such as thinners and cleaning fluids may be inhaled from a cloth or a part of the sniffer's clothing. Aerosols may be sniffed from bags, but are often sprayed directly into the mouth. Sometimes the user may put his head right into a large plastic bag containing solvents.

The effect of sniffing solvents is very much like getting drunk on alcohol, though some sniffers experience hallucinations too. Because the substances used enter the bloodstream through the lungs rather than the stomach, they take effect more quickly than alcohol; if the sniffer wants to stay 'high', he will need to keep sniffing – and will sober up quickly once he stops.

The substances involved contain a wide variety of chemicals, in forms (and with additives) that were never intended for human consumption. Inhalation can affect the heart, making it more sensitive to exertion or excitement, and this may be the reason for some of the sudden deaths that have occurred among sniffers. For this reason, it is unwise to subject sniffers to stress during or immediately after sniffing. Chasing after sniffers could obviously be dangerous. The frightening hallucinations that sometimes result from sniffing solvents could also cause the sniffer's body to release adrenaline, which stimulates the heart, and this could be the cause of some sudden deaths associated with sniffing.

Sniffing itself carries other dangers. Many sniffers choose hazardous surroundings such as derelict buildings, and the sniffer may fall or do something risky while under the influence of solvents. Because the substances used are highly inflammable, there is a danger of the user setting fire to himself or his surroundings, particularly if he is smoking. If plastic bags are used, the user may suffocate if he becomes unconscious, or choke on his own vomit. If aerosols or butane are sprayed directly into the mouth, they can cause swelling of the mouth and throat, blocking the airway and causing suffocation.

Rarely, long-term damage to the lungs, heart, kidneys, liver or central nervous system may result from sniffing. In a few cases, highly toxic substances such as the lead in leaded petrol have caused sniffers permanent brain damage, or other serious and irreversible consequences.

Physical dependence is not thought to be a problem of solvent abuse. Psychological dependence may develop in a few users, usually where there are persistent family or personality problems.

Cannabis

Cannabis is freely available and relatively cheap, and is probably the most widely used of the illegal drugs. It may be supplied as dried leaves, either loose or compressed into blocks, or as a brown resin. It is usually combined with tobacco and rolled into a cigarette, but may also be smoked in a pipe or added to food or drink.

The effects of cannabis in average doses are generally very mild. The user may feel relaxed and sociable, and enjoy a deeper appreciation of experiences such as sound, colour and taste. Someone who is high on cannabis may appear slightly drunk. Higher doses may cause confusion, forgetfulness and distortion of the user's sense of time and reality. Occasionally, the user may become very distressed and confused. These effects will usually wear off within a few hours, although they may persist for longer if the drug has been eaten or drunk.

Cannabis does not produce tolerance or physical dependence, but habitual users may come to rely on the drug as a social aid, rather in the way that many people regard a drink or two as an almost indispensable part of an evening with friends.

Smoking cannabis carries a higher risk of respiratory disease, including lung cancer, than tobacco smoking. Apart from this, most authorities believe that occasional cannabis use is no more dangerous than the moderate use of alcohol or tobacco, although temporary psychological disturbance can result from heavy use and existing mental conditions may be exaggerated. Exceptionally heavy, regular users who are almost permanently intoxicated may be lethargic and unable to perform as they should at school or work. Fatal overdose is virtually impossible.

Amphetamines (speed, uppers)

Most of the illegal amphetamine available to young people is in the form of tablets, or a powder usually composed of a low percentage of amphetamine adulterated (cut) with other, less powerful stimulants like caffeine or ephedrine, or with 'fillers' like glucose powder. This powder is usually sniffed, but can be injected. Less commonly, amphetamine powders can be smoked, or dissolved in water and taken by mouth.

Amphetamines are stimulants. Taken as tablets by mouth and in relatively low doses, they produce a feeling of exhilaration and power, increased energy and capacity to concentrate, enhanced confidence, and the ability to go without sleep or food for long periods. Physical effects can include a rise in blood pressure, increased breathing and heart rate, widening of the pupils, dryness of the mouth, diarrhoea and increased urination. At higher doses, the user may become very talkative, and possibly aggressive, and may appear to be flushed and sweating.

Even at low doses, users can suffer from 'amphetamine psychosis', a condition characterized by extreme mood swings, irritability, and bouts of uncontrolled and possibly violent behaviour. Although the psychosis fades once the drug has left the body, usually after a few days of abstinence, it is followed by a rebound effect of extreme tiredness, depression and anxiety, which may last for days or weeks.

Overdose can result in muscle spasms, a racing pulse and a high temperature. A severe overdose can result in convulsions, coma and, rarely, death from heart failure, collapse of blood vessels in the brain or extremely high fever. Most deaths associated with amphetamine use, however, are associated with the more general risks of injecting any drug.

Amphetamines do not cause physical dependence or withdrawal symptoms, although users quickly become tolerant and need increasingly large doses to achieve the same effects, but it can be very difficult to stop using amphetamines once the user has experienced the sense of energy and well-being induced by the drug, particularly if he is finding life a bit of a struggle. The relapse rate is high among regular amphetamine users who do manage to stop.

Cocaine

Cocaine, usually supplied either in the form of a crystalline white powder or rocky lumps called 'crack', is a stimulant with properties similar to amphetamines. In its powder form, it is most commonly sniffed through a tube into the nose, where it is quickly absorbed into the blood. More rarely, it is injected, but is likely to damage skin tissue and cause ulcers. Both powdered and crack cocaine can be smoked, either in cigarettes or pipes mixed with tobacco or, more commonly, using a water pipe. Users often make their own pipes using drinks cans, plastic or glass bottles or drinking glasses, foil and tubing, heating the drug with a match or cigarette lighter.

The effects of using cocaine are very much like those of amphetamines – a feeling of strength and energy, excitement and talkativeness, and a decreased need for food and sleep. Pupils may be dilated and the eyes more sensitive than usual to bright light. Large doses can cause anxiety, aggression and even hallucinations, which usually wear off once the drug has left the system.

After use and as the drug wears off, the user will feel tired, drowsy and depressed, although these effects are not as great as those associated with amphetamine use. Physical dependence with withdrawal symptoms is not a problem for cocaine users, even regular ones, but strong psychological dependence is likely for the regular user.

Repeated sniffing can cause ulceration and damage to the nose. Besides the increased risk of abscesses and skin damage and the risks associated with injecting any drug, cocaine supplies may often be adulterated with substances that can be harmful if injected. Overdose is possible, and can cause death from heart or respiratory failure, but is fairly unusual.

Ecstasy (MDMA)

Methylenedioxymethamphetamine is a combined stimulant (amphetamine) and hallucinogenic drug, although at commonly used doses it does not normally produce hallucinations in the way that LSD, for instance, does. It comes in tablet or capsule form, and is taken exclusively by mouth. Ecstasy is essentially a social drug, and is widely used by young people to enable them to sustain energetic dancing for long periods without exhaustion.

Ecstasy has effects similar to amphetamines, with the addition of a heightening of awareness which users say increases their enjoyment of an evening's dancing with friends. The drug begins to take effect between 20–60 minutes after taking the pill or capsule. Pupils become dilated, the jaw tightens, and there may be a brief feeling of nausea, sweating, a dry mouth, a rise in blood pressure and loss of appetite. Co-ordination can be impaired. When the drug wears off, the user may experience the same sort of rebound effects that are associated with amphetamines – tiredness, depression, and aches and pains that may last for several days.

There have been a number of ecstasy-related deaths in the United Kingdom, mainly attributed to a rare reaction to the drug causing respiratory failure, although heart failure and brain haemorrhage have also been reported. More common are less serious problems including fits, headaches and various unexplained pains. Because they are able to dance more energetically and for longer after taking the drug, users may suffer from the effects of heat-stroke, dehydration and exhaustion, which can be at least partly avoided by drinking plenty of fluids. Some users have reported hallucinations, panic, confusion and insomnia, and there is some evidence that MDMA use may be associated with liver damage, and also affect the immune system.

MDMA is not physically addictive. It may, however, be

difficult for a user to stop using the drug while continuing to take part in the related social scene.

Opiates

Opiates include heroin, morphine, opium and methadone, and are derived from the opium poppy, although there are now synthetic substitutes. They can be taken by mouth, but may also be sniffed, smoked or injected. Heroin, the most widely used illicit opiate, is most popularly used by heating the powder and inhaling the smoke through a small tube.

Opiates have a depressant and calming effect on the user. They effectively cushion him from the effects of anxiety, fear and discomfort and reduce the desire for food and sex, giving the feeling of being 'wrapped in cotton wool'. They will suppress the cough reflex and they slow respiration and heart rate, dilate blood vessels, and cause sweating and narrowing of the pupils. They do little direct harm to the body in moderate doses, even with long-term use, although fatal overdose is possible. Illegal drugs are always an unknown quantity, however, and it is not uncommon for street heroin to be adulterated with substances that can cause fatal reactions if injected, or to be unexpectedly pure and lead to accidental overdose.

The major danger to opiate users arises from the lifestyle that goes with regular drug use, and from the dangers associated with injecting drugs. People who use opiates regularly may become apathetic and neglect themselves. The need to ensure a daily supply of drugs in order to avoid withdrawal may lead the user to resort to crime, prostitution or some other risky means to finance his or her habit. Regular heroin sniffing can cause damage to the nose.

Opiates are highly addictive. Tolerance and physical dependence develop quickly with repeated use, so that the user must take higher and higher doses and adopt more direct routes of administration to achieve the same effect. Addicts will experience unpleasant withdrawal symptoms including sweating, anxiety, muscle cramps, fever and diarrhoea if they stop taking the drug, and the reaction can be severe enough to be fatal in a very heavy regular user. After a while, the heavy user will cease to experience the pleasurable effects of the drug, but will need to take it regularly just to avoid the unpleasantness of withdrawal and to feel 'normal'.

LSD (lysergic acid diethylamide)

LSD is normally supplied as an impregnated square of paper or gelatine, often printed with cartoon characters or colourful patterns, or made into tablets (usually very small) or capsules. It is taken exclusively by mouth.

A moderate dose of LSD will produce intensification and distortion of the senses. The user may 'see' sounds and 'hear' colours, his surroundings may seem to shift and change, and his sense of time may be distorted, but he is usually aware that these distortions are not real. While many 'trips' are harmless or pleasant, some may be frightening and depressing, particularly if the user was feeling anxious or unhappy before taking the drug. It is possible, though rare, that a user might injure himself or others while gripped by a hallucination – there have been a few well-publicized incidents of people throwing themselves off buildings under the influence of LSD, convinced that they could fly, or attacking others, believing that they are themselves being threatened or attacked. Some users have remained psychologically disturbed after a bad trip long after the drug itself has worn off, although this again is rare.

LSD acts mainly on the mind, and physical dependence does not arise, even with long-term use. Tolerance builds up very rapidly, to the point where the drug becomes ineffective after a few days' use, and the user has to stop for at least three or four days before using it again. Psychological dependence is very rare.

Ketamine

Ketamine is an anaesthetic with hallucinogenic properties, and comes as tablets, liquid or powder. It can cause experiences similar to LSD, with the same possibly dangerous consequences, but has additional effects on the body including loss of sensation, breathing problems and unconsciousness. Mixing ketamine with other drugs or alcohol is particularly dangerous.

Tranquillizers

Benzodiazepines such as temazepam, lorazepam and diazepam (marketed as Valium, Librium, Ativan and Mogadon, among others) are tranquillizing drugs prescribed to relieve anxiety or help the patient to sleep. Most are marketed in the form of pills or capsules containing powder, with the exception of temazepam, which also comes as a capsule containing gel.

In non-anxious individuals these drugs may have very little pleasurable effect, although Valium (a minor tranquillizer) can sometimes produce a mild euphoria. Because of this, they are unlikely to appeal to a new drug user, although their presence in the drug market means that they may sometimes be sold to inexperienced and undiscriminating teenagers.

Tolerance to and serious dependency on these drugs develops with repeated use, and discontinuation can produce withdrawal symptoms including irritability, nausea, insomnia, and even convulsions. Extremely heavy users who stop taking benzodiazepines *abruptly* can die of the effects of withdrawal, and should only stop under medical supervision. If these drugs are taken with other drugs, especially alcohol, fatal overdose is possible.

Barbiturates (barbs, sleepers)

Like the benzodiazepines, barbiturates such as Tuinal, Seconal and Amytal have been used medically in the treatment of anxiety and to help the patient to sleep. Because they carry a very high risk of fatal overdose, they have been largely replaced in the treatment of all but the most severe cases by the safer benzodiazepines, and are now little used medically and therefore not widely available to illicit users.

Small doses of barbiturate help the user to relax, but higher doses have effects very similar to drunkenness – slurred speech, lack of co-ordination and, ultimately, unconsciousness. Tolerance to the drug develops quickly, so the user needs to take more to get the desired sedative effect, but the margin between an effective and a fatal dose is very small, so that overdosing is a very real danger. This danger is even greater if barbiturates are combined with other drugs, especially tranquillizers, alcohol or heroin. Repeated use leads to psychological and physical dependency, and withdrawal is very difficult, with the same symptoms as the benzodiazepines (above). Sudden withdrawal can be fatal for heavy users.

Rohypnol (roofies, R-2)

Like the benzodiazapines and barbiturates, Rohypnol is a sedative drug used medically to treat sleep disorders such as insomnia, and sometimes it is used in minor medical procedures. Its effects are similar to the tranquillizer Valium, but very much stronger. As a prescription drug, it is sold as a white tablet with the manufacturer's name, Roche, written across it. Because it is cheap and easily available, it has become popular with young people and club-goers.

Rohypnol has become infamous as the 'date rape' drug because it dissolves quickly in drinks, becoming undetectable. Mixed with alcohol, it can cause blackouts. The manufacturers have attempted to overcome this problem by making it slower to dissolve, and adding a blue dye to the tablets, but the unmodified form of the drug is still easily available.

Rohypnol takes effect within 20 to 30 minutes and lasts up to eight hours. It induces amnesia, relaxes the muscles, and slows reactions. Tolerance is likely with repeated use, so increased doses are necessary to get the same effect. Physical dependency can result, causing withdrawal symptoms if use is discontinued, and it can be very difficult for a habitual user to give up the drug.

Hallucinogenic mushrooms

There are several varieties of hallucinogenic mushroom (often known as 'magic mushrooms') growing wild in Britain. They can be picked fresh in early autumn, and eaten raw or cooked, brewed into a tea, or dried for later use. Twenty or thirty mushrooms may be required for a hallucinogenic experience similar to a mild dose of LSD, although their potency is very variable.

The user will often suffer stomach pain and vomiting, but the greatest danger to the teenage experimenter is that of eating by mistake one of the highly toxic varieties of fungi that grow wild in Britain; some species can kill if eaten even in very small amounts. It is important that teenagers who live near, or visit, a place where wild fungi grow understand this risk.

Amyl, butyl and isobutyl nitrite (poppers)

Amyl, butyl and isobutyl nitrite (collectively known as alkyl nitrites) are clear, yellow, volatile liquids. They are supplied in small glass bottles with screw or plug tops, or occasionally in small glass capsules wrapped in cotton wool. All substances are inhaled, either straight from the bottle or from a cloth.

Alkyl nitrites dilate the blood vessels and relax muscles, causing a 'rush' as the blood vessels dilate and heartbeat quickens, sending blood to the brain. These effects last only for a few minutes, and result in dizziness, facial flushing and headache. Tolerance develops after two or three weeks of continual use, but abates after a few days without use. Neither physical or psychological dependence, nor withdrawal symptoms, seem to be a problem.

Very heavy use may result in a reduction of oxygen in the blood, which can cause vomiting, shock and unconsciousness. This condition can lead to death, although those cases that have been reported have usually been of people who have swallowed the substance rather than inhaled it. The danger of serious consequences of this sort is greater for anyone with heart trouble or anaemia.

Because the drug leaves the body rapidly after use, there don't seem to be any serious long-term problems arising from the inhalation of nitrites by healthy individuals.

Over-the-counter drugs

Many drugs with abuse potential are available without prescription from pharmacies and other shops. Antihistamines may be used for their sedative effect; the amphetamine-like substances in decongestants may be used as a stimulant, and painkillers, cough linctuses and diarrhoea treatments may be taken in large doses for their opiate content. These practices can be highly dangerous because, in order to obtain the desired effect from the element of the preparation that the user is interested in, it is necessary for him also to take very large doses of its other ingredients – and some of these, such as the paracetamol often combined with codeine in painkillers, can be very damaging indeed.

What else can parents do?

You have armed your child with information about drug use generally, the specific drugs she is most likely to encounter and their effects, and made it clear that you are always willing to talk with her about the issues surrounding drug use and abuse. So what else can you do to help her to make the right choices about drugs?

Many teenagers get drawn into drug use because they feel that everybody is doing it, and they will be left out or ostracized if they don't join in. Parents can help by talking to their teenagers about these feelings, and working with them to develop and rehearse strategies for saying 'no' to drugs – and to other forms of risky behaviour.

It is worth pointing out to your child that research into drug use among young people suggests that although more than 60 per cent have tried cannabis by the time they are 18, fewer than 10 per cent have experimented with 'hard' drugs. Whatever others might suggest, they would certainly not be alone in choosing to avoid recreational drug use.

Dealing with drug use

Since at least 60 per cent of young people are believed to have used cannabis at least once during their teenage years, there is a very strong possibility that your child will be one of them.

What should you do if you suspect that your teenager is using drugs?

- *Keep calm*
  Difficult though it may be if you think you have found evidence of drug use, try to wait until the initial shock and panic have worn off and you can talk calmly to your child. You may be mistaken in your assumptions – and even if you are not, one-off experimentation is very common and the most likely explanation.
- *Choose your moment*
  Don't try to talk to your child while he is under the influence of drugs. Wait until he is sober and you have some time together and can approach the matter calmly.
- *Listen to his side of the story*
  It is more helpful, initially, to ask questions than to make assumptions or give lectures.
- *Don't make drugs the whole issue*
  If your child is using drugs regularly, they are probably only part of a wider problem. Ask how he feels about other things – school, friends, any tensions within the family.
- *Understand that he may not be able to talk to you*
  Offer help, support and advice, but be aware that he may find it easier to talk to someone outside the family (see Useful Addresses).
- *Get help*
  Don't try to cope alone – parenting is a hard job and we all need support sometimes. (See Useful Addresses for sources of support for parents.)

For those readers who want to know more about drugs, see my *Everything Parents Should Know About Drugs* (Sheldon Press, 1995).

Useful Addresses

ADFAM
www.adfam.org.uk

Waterbridge House
32–36 Loman Street
London SE1 0EH
Tel.: 020 7928 8898
Helpline: 020 7928 8900
E-mail: admin@adfam.org.uk

Information and support for families of drug users.

Advisory Centre for Education (ACE)
www.ace-ed.org.uk

Department A
Unit 1C Aberdeen Studios
22 Highbury Grove
London N5 2DQ
Advice line: 0808 800 5793 (Monday–Friday 2 p.m.–5 p.m.)
E-mail: ace-ed@easynet.org.uk

News and information for parents, school governors and teachers. ACE produce many useful leaflets and publications, including: *Appealing for a School*, *Tackling Bullying*, *Getting Extra Help* and *Exclusion*.

Anti-Bullying Campaign
www.bullying.co.uk

185 Tower Bridge Road
London SE1 2UF
Tel.: 020 7378 1446

Telephone support service (Monday–Friday 10 a.m.–4 p.m.) for parents

Careline: Confidential telephone counselling for children, young people and adults, tel.: 020 8514 1177

This organization produces factsheets and guidelines for teachers, parents and children.

British Association for Counselling and Psychotherapy
www.bacp.co.uk

1 Regent Place
Rugby
Warwickshire CV21 2PJ
Tel.: 0870 443 5252
E-mail: bacp@bacp.co.uk

Information about counselling and practising counsellors.

Brook Advisory Centres
www.brook.org.uk

Unit 421
Highgate Studios
52–79 Highgate Road
London NW5 1TL
Tel.: 020 7284 6040

Free, confidential sexual health advice, contraception and counselling for young people up to the age of 25.

ChildLine
www.childline.org.uk

Call 0800 1111, or write to Freepost 1111, London N1 0BR

Free United Kingdom helpline for children and young people. It provides a confidential phone counselling service for any child or young person with any problem 24 hours a day. The lines can be busy, so please keep trying.

Children's Legal Centre
www2.essex.ac.uk/clc

The Children's Legal Centre
University of Essex
Wivenhoe Park
Colchester
Essex CO4 3SQ

Advice line: 01206 873820 (Monday–Friday 10 a.m.–12.30 p.m. and 2 p.m.–4.30 p.m.)
E-mail: clc@essex.ac.uk

An independent national charity concerned with the law and policy affecting children and young people. It has an extensive publications list and a legal query service.

Contact-a-Family
www.cafamily.org.uk

209–211 City Road
London EC1V 1JN
Tel.: 020 7608 8700
Minicom: 020 7608 8702

Freephone helpline for parents and families: 0808 808 3555 (Monday–Friday 10 a.m.–4 p.m.)
E-mail: info@cafamily.org.uk

A charity helping families who care for children with any disability or special need.

Department for Education and Skills
Sanctuary Buildings
Great Smith Street
London SW1P 3BT
Public enquiries: 0870 000 2288
Minicom: 020 7925 6873
E-mail: info@dfes.gsi.gov.uk
DfES parents' website: www.dfes.gov.uk

Offers a huge amount of information on every aspect of school.

DfES Publications Centre
PO Box 5050
Sudbury
Suffolk CO10 6ZQ

For written information on many aspects of education. Write for a publications list, see the DfES website for parents (www.dfes.gov.uk/parents) or ring the orderline on 0845 6022260.

Eating Disorders Association
www.edauk.com

103 Prince of Wales Road
Norwich NR1 1DW
Adult helpline: 0845 634 1414 (Monday–Friday 8.30 a.m.–8.30 p.m.)
Youthline: 0845 634 7650 (Monday–Friday 4 p.m.–6.30 p.m.)
Text-phone service: 01603 753322 (Monday–Friday 8.30 a.m.–8.30 p.m.)
E-mail: info@edauk.com

Confidential support and information for anyone in the United Kingdom.

Association of Professional Piercers (APP)
PO Box 16044
London NW1 8ZD
Tel.: 0117 9603923

Runs a voluntary register of ear and body-piercers.

Family Planning Association
www.fpa.org.uk

2–12 Pentonville Road
London N1 9FP
Tel.: 020 7837 5432
Helpline: 0845 310 1334 (Monday–Friday 9 a.m.–7 p.m.)

Information on contraception, sex and relationships, abortion, sexual health, and sexually transmitted diseases. The FPA publishes a wide range of booklets and resource packs for young people and parents.

Family 2000 Onwards
www.family2000onwards.com

Information and support site for parents, grandparents and

children concerning divorce. Includes articles on all aspects of family life, and reviews of books for parents.

FFLAG (Families and Friends of Lesbians and Gays)
www.fflag.org.uk
PO Box No. 84
Exeter EX4 4AN
Central helpline: 01454 852418
E-mail: info@fflag.org.uk

Supports parents and their gay, lesbian and bisexual sons and daughters. Has a network of local parents groups and contacts.

Institute of Family Therapy
www.instituteoffamilytherapy.org.uk
24–32 Stephenson Way
London NW1 2HX
Tel.: 020 7391 9150

Mediation and negotiation service for families, couples and other relationship groups.

Kidscape
www.kidscape.org.uk
2 Grosvenor Gardens
London SW1W 0DH
Tel.: 020 7730 3300

Send a large SAE for bullying information pack.
Parents' bullying helpline: 08451 205 204 (local rate) (Monday–Friday 10 a.m.–4 p.m.)

National Drugs Helpline
www.ndh.org.uk
Tel.: 0800 776600

Drug information and advice helpline.

National Children's Bureau
www.ncb.org.uk

8 Wakley Street
London EC1V 7QE
Tel.: 020 7843 6000

A charity that promotes the interests and well-being of all children and young people. Offers: publications, conferences, library and information services.

National Family and Parenting Institute
www.nfpi.org.uk

430 Highgate Studios
53–79 Highgate Road
London NW5 1TL
Tel.: 020 7424 3460
E-mail: info@nfpi.org

An independent charity working to enhance the value and quality of family life. Publications on child-rearing and the family.

Parents Information Network
www.pin.org.uk

Information and advice for parents whose children are using computers and the internet. Security, protection from viruses, and the use of software to filter out unwanted material.

Parentline Plus
www.parentlineplus.org.uk

520 Highgate Studios
53–79 Highgate Road
Kentish Town
London NW5 1TL
Tel.: 0808 800 2222
Text phone: 0800 783 6783

Charity offering support to anyone parenting a child – parents, stepparents, grandparents and foster parents. Freephone helpline, broad range of publications, and courses for parents.

Release
www.release.org.uk

388 Old Street
London EC1V 9LT
Advice line: 020 7729 9904 (Monday–Friday 10 a.m.–6 p.m.)
24-hour emergency line: 020 7603 8654
Drugs in schools: 0345 366666 (Monday–Friday 10 a.m.–5 p.m.)
E-mail: info@release.org.uk

Information and legal advice on drugs and the problems arising from them.

Trust for the Study of Adolescence
www.tsa.uk.com

23 New Road
Brighton BN1 1WZ
Tel.: 01273 693311
E-mail: info@tsa.uk.com

Information about adolescence and adolescents, for parents, young people and professionals.

YoungMinds
www.youngminds.org.uk

102–108 Clerkenwell Road
London EC1M 5SA
Tel.: 020 7336 8445
Parents' information service: 0800 018 2138
E-mail: enquiries@youngminds.org.uk

National charity committed to improving the mental health of all children and young people. Confidential information and advice for any adult with concerns about the mental health of a child or young person.

Youth Access
2a Taylors Yard
67 Alderbrook Road
London SW12 8AD
Tel.: 020 8772 9900
E-mail: admin@youthaccess.org.uk

Gives details of local counselling and advice centres for young people.

Further Reading

Baker, Carol, *Getting On With Your Children*. Longman, 1990.

Figes, Kate, *The Terrible Teens; What Every Parent Needs to Know*. Penguin, 2002.

Holt, John, *How Children Fail*. Penguin, 1990.

Holt, John, *How Children Learn*. Penguin, 1991.

Lawson, Sarah, *Helping Children Cope with Bullying*. Sheldon Press, 1994.

Lawson, Sarah, *Everything Parents Should Know About Drugs*. Sheldon Press, 1995.

Lindenfield, Gael, *Confident Teens: How to Raise a Positive, Confident and Happy Teenager*. HarperCollins, 2001.

Quinn, Kaleghl, *Everyday Self-defence: Protect Yourself with Attitude, Intuition and Strategy*. HarperCollins, 1993.

Index

opposite sex relationships:
dating 104–6; early days
of 74–5; 'just friends' 75

parents: 'because I say so'
35; dealing with mistakes
82–3; homework help
38–41; imperfect 20–1;
lone 19–20; marriage
strains 29; own
experiences as teens 29;
talking about sex 101–2
parties 81–2
peer group: disability and
76; girls 69; importance
of 68; parties 82–3
peer groups: boys'
friendships 68–9; places
for socializing 69–71;
pressure from 73–4;
setting boundaries 71–3
personal appearance: body-
piercing 24–5; conformity
22–3; hair 23–4; tattooing
25
pregnancy 3
privacy 72; doctors and
66–7; lying 18;
possessions and rooms
16–18
puberty: boys 3–5; defining
1; early and late 7–8;
emotional and mental
effects 8–11; girls 1–3

rebellion 87–8
relationships: changes during
puberty 9–10 *see also*

family; opposite sex
relationships; peer groups;
sex
responsibility: helping
decision-making 26–30

school: and bullying 46–8;
difficulties of 31–2;
feedback 41; homework
37–41; nurse 113; reasons
for 32–5; Sex and
Relationships Education
99–101; signs of bullying
44; stress from 41–2;
teachers as bullies 48–9
self-esteem: effects of
bullying 45; and school
33
sex and sexuality 98–9;
clinics 112–13, 115;
contraception 110–13;
dating 104–6; drugs/
drinking and 118;
emotions and 103–4;
exploitation and abuse
108–9; and homosexuality
106–8, 110; and the law
109–10; onset of puberty
and 3, 5; parental
discussion of 101–2; Sex
and Relationships
Education 99–101 *see also*
opposite sex relationships
sexually transmitted infection
(STI): doctors and 67;
HIV/AIDS 115–16; types
and signs of 114–15
skin 6; body image and 8;

care of problems 65–6
sleep: changes in puberty
6–7; effects of bullying
44–5
smoking 117, 120
stress: causes 58; coping
with 58–9; from school
41–2

suicide 61–3

teenagers: defining
adolescence 1
toxic shock syndrome 3

Youth Counselling Service
61